The CR FAQ

The CR FAQ

An Introduction to
Celtic Reconstructionist Paganism

by

Kathryn Price NicDhàna, Erynn Rowan Laurie,
C. Lee Vermeers, Kym Lambert ní Dhoireann,
and other members of the CR community

River House Publishing
Leverett, Massachusetts, USA

River House Publishing
P.O. Box 734
Leverett, Massachusetts 01054 USA

Printed in the United States of America
11 10 09 08 07   9 8 7 6 5 4 3 2 1

First Printing: August, 2007

Cover, back, and all art Copyright ©2007 Kathryn Price NicDhàna

This edition is published as an adjunct
to the original web document at
http://www.paganachd.com/faq
Errata and updates will be posted to the website.

Paperback ISBN-13: 978-0-6151-5800-6

Introduction

Welcome to *The CR FAQ - An Introduction to Celtic Reconstructionist Paganism.*

While no one individual speaks for the CR community as a whole, it is through consensus documents such as this one that we endeavour to present the core, shared principles, beliefs and practices of our community. This document is presented in the form of a FAQ: answers to **F**requently **A**sked **Q**uestions about Celtic Reconstructionism.

The CR FAQ was written by a diverse collective of CR elders and long-term practitioners, including some of the founders of the tradition. It was written through a consensus process, using a CeltiWiki database designed for the project. Using a Wiki format meant that all of the core authors were able to co-write and edit one another's work until a consensus answer emerged. The resulting versions of all answers were posted on the *cr_r*[1] online community, enabling over 360 members of the Celtic Reconstructionist community the opportunity to provide input and feedback, much of which was then incorporated. The project was also announced in multiple CR online communities, so those who were interested in contributing could come and join in. Following in the tradition of 2003's *"The CR Essay,"*[2] *The CR FAQ* is only the second defining document co-authored and approved by representatives of multiple, longstanding CR sub-traditions.

This FAQ is meant to provide a variety of viewpoints on CR and an introduction to our community. While no book or website, even a collectively-authored one, can claim to speak for every individual everywhere who identifies as CR, we have made our

---

[1] *http://community.livejournal.com/cr_r/*
[2] *www.witchvox.com/trads/trad_cr.html*

best effort to be inclusive and representative of our diverse community while still making it clear that there are boundaries and limitations on what is considered CR. We hope it will provide a good introduction to our community and tradition and that you enjoy your visit with us. *Fáilte!* (Welcome!)

Some Of Our Assumptions

In this document we have, for the most part, chosen to use Modern Irish as the Celtic language of choice. This is not to indicate that all CR is Irish, but simply because we had to standardize many of our references to *some* language for the sake of readability. We also use Celtic languages for the parts of our beliefs and practices that cannot be expressed in English, and because nurturing and helping to revitalize the Celtic languages is an important part of CR. Hopefully, the importance we place on the Celtic languages is reflected in this document while still making it accessible to those who do not speak any of these languages.

In addition, Modern Irish has the advantage of a standardized spelling system, is perhaps the easiest Celtic language to find classes in, and we have observed more CR-oriented people tending toward Gaelic cultures than Brythonic or Continental ones. However, we've used older spellings in some cases where a word has been incorporated into English or an older spelling is more likely to be understood by the reader. There are also some cases where we use a word from a different Celtic language because it is necessary to use a specific term from that language. In those cases, we have chosen to use whichever spelling seems easiest to understand. Finally, there are a couple of cases in which older spellings are mandated due to long use (such as their usage in the names of traditions or organizations). In those cases, we've used whichever spelling we feel is the most appropriate.

This FAQ tends to assume a basic familiarity with religious concepts and terminology, with the occasional foray into related fields like archeology, anthropology and psychology. We have included a glossary to cover some of the more obscure terms. If a confusing word or phrase is not in the glossary, dictionaries or Internet search engines like Google are always helpful.

Again, *Fáilte!* (Welcome!), and we hope you enjoy your stay with us!

Conventions for the Print Edition:

References to other questions within this document are in **bold** in the body text and bulleted with a ✧ at the end of answers.

Non-English words and phrases are in *italic*.

URLs or hyperlinked phrases in the online edition are indicated by ***italics and bold***. Wording has been altered slightly in some cases to accommodate the print format. Please see the online version of this FAQ at ***http://www.paganachd.com/faq*** for current and up-to-date linkage. A URL (Uniform Resource Locator) is an Internet or web address.

Contents

13

Chapter One

So What is
Celtic Reconstructionism (CR)?

What is Celtic Reconstructionism (CR)?

Celtic Reconstructionist Paganism (CR) is a polytheistic, animistic, religious and cultural movement. It is an effort to reconstruct, within a modern Celtic cultural context, the aspects of ancient Celtic religions that were lost or subsumed by Christianity.

There are some survivals of pre-Christian Celtic traditions in the lore and folk practices of the Celtic countries and the Celtic diaspora but, after centuries of Christian overlay, most people do not find these folk traditions by themselves to be a whole or viable spiritual path. By studying the old manuscript sources and the regional folklore, combining this information with mystical and ecstatic practice, and working together to weed out the non-Celtic elements that can arise, we are nurturing what still lives and helping the polytheistic Celtic traditions grow strong and whole again. We approach this in part by trying to envision what different Celtic Paganisms might look like today if they had been uninterrupted by Christianity, much as Hinduism has changed over the centuries, remaining the same religion but changing in form with the changing times.

What do you mean by "Celtic"?

"Celtic" applies to a group of related languages in the Indo-European (IE) language group and the cultures that developed in the communities that speak these languages. Celtic identity is not based on genetics or "blood" but on being part of this linguistic and cultural grouping. Celtic is pronounced "Keltik" unless you are French, in which case it is "Selteek." Don't ask us about the Boston basketball team or the Glasgow football/soccer club. We have no clue.

CR greatly values the study and preservation of Celtic languages as well as participation in the living Celtic cultures. Language is the key to understanding a culture's mindset. While fluency in a Celtic language is not a prerequisite to participation in the CR community, people serious about developing the tradition almost always dedicate themselves to studying one of the Celtic languages as part of their CR practice.

So what are the Celtic Languages?

There are two basic groupings of Celtic language: Continental and Insular. Each of these are broken down into further divisions of Q-Celtic or P-Celtic. The distinctions between P- and Q-Celtic are made based on the differences like those in the words for "son" and "head" – in Irish, *mac* and *ceann*, and in Welsh, *map* and *pen*.

In Continental Celtic, there were a number of languages: Cisalpine Gaulish (Northern Italy), Transalpine Gaulish (France, Switzerland, Austria, Germany), Galatian (modern Turkey/Anatolia), Lepontic (Northern Italy), and Celtiberian (Spain/Portugal – the only continental Q-Celtic language). These languages are no longer spoken.

In Insular Celtic, there are seven languages known for certain. The Goidelic (Gaelic) Q-Celtic languages are Irish, Scottish, and Manx. The Brythonic (or British) P-Celtic languages are Welsh, Breton, and Cornish, as well as the long-dead Cumbrian language. Pictish seems to be an archaic form of P-Celtic.

What do you mean by "Reconstruction"?

In discussions of religions of antiquity, "reconstruction" refers to the process of building a model of previous historic and pre-historic traditions, and then examining that model for ideas of how to implement those traditions in a modern, practical sense. The specific definition of "reconstruction" which fits our usage best is, "an interpretation formed by piecing together bits of evidence."

In the case of CR, what we are attempting to model are the various forms of pre-Christian Celtic spirituality. We do this in order to create a modern spiritual practice that retains as much authentic older material as possible while also being workable in the modern world. We do this because we feel called to Celtic Deities and a Celtic worldview, and we wish to help preserve modern Celtic languages, music, and cultures.

Is it a new or old tradition?

CR is a new tradition based on old ideas and ideals. We work with the best current scholarship we can find to try to understand the cultures of the early Celtic peoples, and what they were doing in terms of pre-Christian, polytheistic spiritual traditions. We also participate in the traditions of the current, living Celtic cultures in ways that express a polytheistic, animist spirituality. But while many Pagan elements have survived in the living Fairy Faith and other folkloric practices, in terms of a complete, polytheistic, Pagan religion, CR does not have, nor has it ever claimed, any unbroken lineage to the pre-Christian past.

Along with the work of scholarship, we also rely on our own *iomas* and *aisling* – our inspiration and our visionary practices – to help us find ways to integrate old practices into a new time and setting. One of the primary thought-exercises behind the development of CR is "what would the Celtic spiritual cultures look like if they had been uninterrupted by Christianity?" All religions and traditions grow and change with time. If Celtic polytheist cultures had been uninterrupted from the Iron Age until today, they would still look very different from what was being done in the Iron Age, just as Hinduism and other spiritual paths have, over time, changed in their own lands and cultural matrices.

How and when did CR start?

For many years there had been a general dissatisfaction with the popular approaches to Celtic Spirituality, and a number of individuals were in dialogue about how to create a more authentic approach to polytheistic, Celtic religion. Over the 1980s, a growing number of people began coming together to discuss the issue and share information about their Proto-CR practices.

A key event in laying the groundwork for much CR practice was the 1985 Pagan Spirit Gathering in Wisconsin, USA, and its Celtic discussions and workshops. Participants at this gathering returned home and continued to develop the foundations of their CR sub-traditions, incorporating some of the ideas they had shared in person. In later years, some of them would re-meet online and once again collaborate.

The first appearance in print of the term "Celtic Reconstructionist," used to describe a specific religious movement and not just a style of Celtic studies, was by Kym Lambert ní Dhoireann in the Spring, 1992 issue of *Harvest* magazine (Southboro, Massachusetts, USA). Ní Dhoireann credits Kathryn Price NicDhàna with originating the term "Celtic Reconstructionist"; however, NicDhàna credits her early use of the term to a simple extrapolation of Margot Adler's use of the term "Pagan Reconstructionists" in the original, 1979 edition of *Drawing Down the Moon*. Though Adler devotes space to a handful of Reconstructionist traditions, none of those mentioned are specifically Celtic. Also in *Drawing Down the Moon*, while describing his Neo-druidic group, New Reformed Druids of North America (NRDNA), Isaac Bonewits used the phrase "Eclectic Reconstructionist." However, by the time CR became a recognized tradition, this pairing of terms had become oxymoronic, as "Reconstructionism" in the Pagan/polytheist sense had now been defined specifically to exclude "Eclecticism."

NicDhàna and Ní Dhoireann have stated that they coined the term CR specifically to distinguish their practices from those of eclectic traditions like Wicca and the Neo-druidry of the time. Erynn Rowan Laurie also began using the name "Celtic Reconstructionist" at some point in the '90s, though "NeoCeltic" was her initial term of choice. With Ní Dhoireann's popularization of Celtic Reconstructionism in the Pagan press, and then the use of the term by these three individuals on the Internet, "Celtic Reconstructionism" began to be adopted as the name for this developing spiritual tradition.

Who's the leader of CR?

There isn't one. Individual groups may have leadership, though some groups are much more informal. In addition, there are a number of people who have gained respect within the broader CR community for their ideas. However, there is no authority which derives from that respect, and that respect is not usually universal nor absolute. We all work for what we have here.

How do I join CR?

Currently (in 2007), the community is relatively small and spread out. Though some CRs are lucky enough to have an in-person community, there are many more CRs whose main sense of community comes from participation in online forums and email lists. Even those who primarily practice with other CRs in person generally join in the online discussions, as that is currently the fastest and easiest way to collaborate with a wide range of people, and can lead to contacts for forming a local community. A combination of reading, individual research, and participation in CR forums and groups will help you connect with and contribute to the CR tradition.

See also

✧ What can I do to get started? (p. 137)

How can you recreate a culture that's dead?

Celtic culture never died. While Celtic languages have at times been endangered, several of them never completely died out, and Welsh and Scots Gaelic, at least, are showing signs of new growth. Cornish has tenuously returned from language death, with a very few people now speaking it as their first language, and a few more having become fluent in it as a second language. Many of the art forms like music, poetry, literature, visual art and dance continue with great vigor. Most CRs are deeply involved in maintaining these parts of the living cultures.

So, if the culture is living, why do you need to reconstruct it?

What does need to be more fully reconstructed are the pre-Christian, polytheistic forms of ritual and spiritual practice that were lost or subsumed during the Christian era. While we have a significant body of folklore, cosmology and mythology to build upon, it is also taking a good deal of experimentation and research to reconstruct a viable spiritual practice. Opinions as to how much needs to be developed do vary in our communities, with some being satisfied with the simple folkloric practices we already have, others wanting more elaborate theatrical or occult rituals, and still others being concerned with a theological structure. Different types of practices are developing in different branches of the tradition. Much work has been done on this, and it is an ongoing project.

Is this a religion, or a culture?

Both. CR is a polytheistic religion that is based on our understanding of, and participation in, the living Celtic cultures. We see our religion as inseparable from culture.

A primary reason CR developed was because we felt the need to keep Celtic spiritual practices and beliefs as much within the context of Celtic cultures as possible. Calling something "Celtic" means it should be rooted **in the culture** and not in practices and beliefs from **outside** of the culture. The process of applying a Celtic veneer over a core of non-Celtic material is akin to dressing an alien practice in knotwork and tartan; it may look Celtic to those unfamiliar with Celtic ways, but its substance is not. In the 1980s, all the "Celtic" Pagan religions we were coming across were variations on this non-Celtic pattern. We were looking for the depth and internal consistency that comes with a specifically culture-based religion, rather than the scattered and, to us, shallow experience of an eclectic or "universal" spirituality. We needed our religion to be an integrated part of a whole cultural matrix, rather than separating our spiritual lives from our daily lives.

Few CRs live in a completely Celtic society, so we cannot claim that everyone who identifies as CR is part of the living Celtic cultures. However, many CRs are involved in the activities of the Celtic diasporan communities, or in these communities in the Celtic lands. Supporting the cultures from which our traditions arise, and helping them grow and thrive, is symbiotic with Celtic spirituality, regardless of whether we live in a Celtic country or in the diaspora. Our aim is not to exactly resurrect a historical culture, but we do look at historic as well as contemporary Celtic cultures to help understand how to ground our practices and beliefs in our daily lives. It also helps to understand that, while we are working to practice a Celtic religion, being a Celt by the strictest definition is not necessary, just as it is not necessary to be Asian to practice Buddhism, an Asian religion.

There was never one monolithic Celtic culture, so there will probably never be one monolithic CR culture. We are too diverse for that. There were (and are) many Celtic lands, and even within those lands there were a variety of customs, practices and beliefs. It's no surprise that this variety is reflected in CR. Not only are there differences in our religious beliefs, but there are also differences in the customs we choose to adopt from living and historical sources as well as our interpretations of these customs.

In a cultural religion, the importance of custom can sometimes outweigh the importance of belief, so some cultural groups may have members who decide to share certain practices even though their own beliefs behind them might vary. It is often easier for some to agree to a custom than to every specific detail of the beliefs behind it. Those differences in belief might be argued, hopefully in a congenial manner and with good references to support them, but despite any differing interpretations of **why** we do something, the customs we share can bond us all the same.

Most of the people in the living Celtic cultures are Christian, though it is a type of Christianity that is often reasonably harmonious with Celtic Paganism. In this spirit, a large, contemporary Celtic community will probably contain both CRs and Celtic Christians, as well as those of Celtic heritage who follow another religion entirely, or no religion at all. The Pagans and Christians may both pray to Bríde at Her holy well, with the CRs seeing Her as a Goddess, while the Celtic Christians see Her as a saint. For us, this is not a conflict. We are all part of the broader tapestry of the living Celtic cultures.

See also

✧ Is Celtic Christianity a part of CR? (p. 132)

But, what do you mean by "The living Celtic cultures"?

When people in the six Celtic nations and the diaspora use this phrase, it can have a few different shadings of meaning.

In the strictest definition, "the living Celtic cultures" refers only to the cultures lived by the people who have grown up speaking a Celtic language, in a community that still has that language as their primary or co-primary language.

In looser usage, it can also refer to the cultures of those who speak a Celtic language to a much lesser extent, but who still maintain the traditional attitudes, customs, beliefs and artforms of the Celtic people who are more immersed in that language and culture. Usually these people are the children or grandchildren of those who did speak the languages, and though they may not have learned a Celtic language in their household while growing up, the culture of their family has not yet had a chance to drift too far away from its roots.

Some people of Celtic heritage, whether living in the Celtic nations or the diaspora, also consider themselves a part of the living culture, even if they don't speak a Celtic language. In these cases, their identification with Celtic culture may be largely an ethnic thing, but it usually involves at the very least the participation in Celtic cultural events, and some degree of respect for the languages, even if they may not be active students.

In CR, when we use the phrase, "living Celtic cultures," we are usually referring to the stricter definition, which, as these things are not always defined by rigid boundaries, can at times fade into the second.

So, everyone in this community calls themselves Celtic Reconstructionists?

Yes and No.

Though most of us refer to our traditions as "Celtic Reconstructionist," and there is a core set of shared principles and some shared ritual structures, in many ways CR is an umbrella term for a variety of sub-traditions.

In the eighties and early nineties, a variety of names were in use for the early approaches to the tradition. In retrospect, many of those things are now referred to as "Proto-CR."

Even after "Celtic Reconstructionism" or "Celtic Reconstructionist Paganism" gradually became the most common term, there have always been other names in use as well. Some CRs choose to apply more cultural specificity in their names, for instance, referring to themselves as "Gaelic Reconstructionists," "Scottish Reconstructionists" or "Welsh Reconstructionists."

Not all people who make use of Neopagan reconstructionist techniques are entirely comfortable with using "Celtic Reconstructionism" as a name for their religion, seeing the term as describing a methodology rather than a system of belief, or seeing the term as being incorrectly descriptive. Others feel comfortable with the term CR, but have decided to name their CR sub-traditions so as to distinguish their practices from other sub-groups and flavors of CR. Some other names that people involved in CR-style religion have chosen to use include:

Amldduwiaeth ("Polytheism" in Welsh)
Aurrad ("Member of the Tribe" in Old Irish)
Celtic Restorationism
Ildiachas ("Polytheism" in Irish Gaelic)
Ioma-Dhiadhachd ("Polytheism" in Scots Gaelic)
Liesdoueadegezh ("Polytheism" in Breton)
Pàganachd ("Paganism, Heathenism" in Scots Gaelic)
Págánacht ("Paganism, Heathenism" in Irish Gaelic)
Págántacht (alternate, and more common, Irish Gaelic spelling of *Págánacht*)
Senistrognata ("Ancestral Customs" in reconstructed Old Celtic)
Yljeeaghys ("Polytheism" in Manx Gaelic)

Chapter Two

Basic Questions

Don't you have to be Irish/Scottish/Welsh to be a Celtic Reconstructionist?

No. You don't have to be Asian to be a Buddhist, either. Practicing a Celtic religion doesn't mean you have to have Celtic ancestry any more than practicing an Asian religion means you must have Asian ancestry. "Celtic" is a language/cultural grouping, not one based on "blood."

Though many people of Celtic heritage are drawn to CR, being of "Celtic descent" is not required. We give respect to all of our ancestors and teachers, whether or not they were Celts. Knowing that humanity originated on the African continent, we believe that we are all of one blood and one human family. CR as a whole is strongly anti-racist and welcomes people of all races, ethnicities and colors who wish to follow Celtic Deities in a CR way.

The Deities call whom They will, and it's not our business to say which Gods and Goddesses you can follow based on the color of your skin, eyes or hair, or the percentage of your blood, if any, that hails from the Celtic lands. Anyone discriminating based on these things is not practicing CR, despite any claims they may make to the contrary.

However, it is important to remember that CR does not happen in a vacuum. Being CR requires involvement in community and culture – both the CR community and the living Celtic cultures, whether in the Celtic nations or in the diaspora.

See also
✧ What do you mean by "Celtic"? (p. 18)

✧ How can you claim to be a Celtic tradition if you're not immersed in the Culture? (p. 28)
✧ How can you recreate a culture that's dead? (p. 21)

How can you claim to be a Celtic tradition if you're not immersed in the Culture?

Many of us are deeply involved in modern Celtic cultures. We participate in language study and preservation, Celtic music, and physical disciplines like dance or various Celtic martial arts forms which come from living traditions or are reconstructed from manuals. Some CRs study traditional recipes and other householder traditions like weaving and traditional dyeing. A number of us are or have been involved in some of the political struggles in the Celtic nations. Many of us live in households with other CRs or with family members who may not be strictly CR but do participate in other Celtic cultural activities such as Irish festivals, *seisiúns*, Highland Games and *cèilidhs*.

As we are not historical re-enactors, no one really lives in Iron Age Celtic culture anymore and (as stated elsewhere) that is not our goal. We are interested in living in a modern Celtic culture, whether in the Celtic lands or in the diaspora, where we participate in the parts of the cultures that never died out and immerse ourselves in our work of reconstructing what was lost or fragmented. Our lives are filled with offerings to the spirits, songs and poetry in Gaelic or Welsh, and an existence which is fully permeated by our contact with the Celtic Deities, our diverse ancestors, and our local nature spirits.

However, as CR grows, there is a certain degree of diversity, and a variety of approaches encompassed under the broader umbrella of CR. There are other members of the CR community who do many of these things from time to time, but do not desire as much immersion. Not everyone in the CR community has the same degree of focus or delighted obsession. There are many CRs who enjoy an urban, multicultural lifestyle, and who just happen to have CR as their religion. And while we encourage as much participation in the living cultures as possible, both sorts of CRs, and those at all points on the spectrum between, are welcome to participate in the CR community.

Do you have a Celtic holy book like the Bible? If there's no central text, how do you know what to believe?

There is no one central text that tells us how to be CR. The early Celtic cultures were oral, and the druids apparently had restrictions on writing down many things that were considered sacred. That said, some aspects of pre-Christian belief did filter through into the monasteries where the earliest Celtic language books were written. Tales were sometimes altered slightly to make them conform better to Christian ideology and cosmology, and recorded that way for future generations.

What we do have are collections of tales that provide much of the basic lore. We also have surviving legal texts, wisdom texts like *The Instructions of Cormac*, and other sources like scholarly analyses of these materials.

These things are supplemented by archaeological and other studies of the physical remains of pre-Christian Celtic cultures, showing us the shapes of daily lives, temple areas, and the workshops of artisans. Another major source for our spiritual paths comes from folkloric traditions still actively practiced in living, modern Celtic communities.

Because we have no one central authority, we have many ways of approaching the material and our practices; however, it's very important to us that what we do is in accord with what we know of historical Celtic practices and beliefs. Only when we do not have firm source material on these things do we consider going to other sources for inspiration and guidance in fleshing out modern CR.

See also
✧ What is the Celtic lore, and where can I find it? (p. 41)
✧ So how do I find this stuff? (p. 154)

If they didn't write anything down, how do you know what they believed?

That depends on who you mean by "they." It is possible that the druids had restrictions on writing down anything that was considered sacred. However, some of the Celtic peoples did leave records of their beliefs and practices, and some of these traditions have survived, in a modified form, up to the present day.

Observers among the Greeks and Romans have left many accounts and commentaries regarding Celtic peoples in ancient Classical literature. However, it is important to bear in mind that these external observers usually had their own agendas, whether political or religious. From these accounts, we know that some Celtic peoples believed in some form of reincarnation or immortality of the soul. We have accounts of them swearing oaths by land, sea and sky. Gaulish ethical precepts are recorded. We know the names of Deities from altar inscriptions, as well as details of some Celtic peoples' beliefs about magic from incidental inscriptions on artifacts such as spell tablets, which have been found on both the continent and the islands. The Coligny calendar preserves a Gaulish view of time, holy days, and what constitutes lucky and unlucky days for activities.

With the arrival of Christianity, we see traces of earlier Pagan beliefs in what was forbidden in the Penitential texts. These are full of proscriptions against the worship of trees and various magical and ritual acts that must have been common among pre-Christian Celtic peoples; otherwise there would have been no need to forbid them. Certain aspects of Paganism also infiltrated early Celtic Christianity, and much of the role of the druids was carried on by the *filí* (poets) in Ireland. We also have law texts from Ireland regarding the roles and status of druids and *filí* that can be quite revealing if studied carefully.

The legal texts of Ireland also preserve information about Celtic Paganism through their reliance on legal precedent – earlier, mythic cases that became the basis of later judicial decisions. The law texts preserve many tales of Pagan times and rely upon Pagan legal decisions as a basis for later judgments. One monastic text preserves a healing spell with appeals to Dian Cécht, the Irish God of healing and Goibhniu, a smith-God. Additionally, Saint Brighid carried many of the attributes of the earlier Goddess Brighid and Her life stories suggest some things that earlier Pagans believed about Her (things which can be confirmed by cross-cultural studies).

Because Celtic cultures were oral, some things were preserved in the storytelling traditions and song. The *Carmina Gadelica*, compiled in the late 19th and early 20th centuries by Alexander Carmichael, preserves a good deal of lore and magic from Scotland. Though much of the material is Catholic, there are earlier layers of Pagan material beneath that, and the appendices include beliefs about auguries and omens as well as healing and spoken spellcraft.

Folk patterns of pilgrimage to holy sites often include sacred springs, caves, and mountains that were holy before the arrival of Christianity. Well-dressing and the practice of tying strips of cloth on trees as an appeal for healing or luck is very likely a survival of pre-Christian Celtic belief. Although we don't have enough to make a full and rounded system of Pagan belief from the fragments that survived, there is a great deal for us to work from. With the addition of evidence from archaeology and linguistic studies, and the help of comparative studies of religion and mythology as well as cultural anthropology and Indo-European studies, CR works to restore what was lost and bring things forward for new generations.

How do you pick which authors to believe?

There are two approaches. One is to find well-read, experienced and knowledgeable people to recommend books to you. In order for this to work, they must be people you trust to make correct judgments between good and bad research. CR folk often debate the validity and accuracy of information presented in books. Usually an eventual consensus judgment emerges about the author or book.

The second approach is a difficult but very personally rewarding learning process of developing that discerning judgment yourself. This involves critical thinking and the ability to discern the difference between fantasy and reality, solid attributed research and wishful thinking. It's useful to go through the bibliography of any book you are looking at. Check out who is writing the books the author references. If most of the books in the bibliography are printed by occult and Pagan presses, chances are you're better off looking at a different source. However, if a book or article is published by an academic press – affiliated with a university or other academic institution – you're more likely to find useful and accurate information.

A crucial point in evaluating any book is whether the author is writing within their own field of expertise. For instance, someone with an advanced degree in archaeology, but no training in the Celtic languages, might be invaluable in terms of understanding sacred sites, but next to worthless in analyzing the mythology. A Ph.D. level zoologist might be a fine author on zoology, but know absolutely nothing about Celtic studies or comparative mythology. If an author cannot read the original language of the texts they are using as source materials, there are bound to be flaws in their interpretation. Similarly, if an author is trained in Classical and European mythology, but is not an expert on the Insular Celts, their conclusions will be filtered through a different lens and may easily result in a warped view.

We cannot believe any authors who write on matters Celtic if what they are presenting is based on nothing more than their own opinion. Checking their references is absolutely necessary if you are uncertain as to the historical accuracy of their work. If you can't find credible sources with some proof of their claims, it's best to take the information with a grain of salt or to regard it as personal opinion, not fact. The most accurate sources on Celtic history and religion are going to be archaeologists, Celtic historians, and language experts publishing through academic presses, not occult and New Age authors. The books may be more difficult to wade through, but the rewards for doing so are immense.

Is there a certain era that you focus on reconstructing?

As we're not a historical recreation society, there isn't an "era" to focus on. The Celtic traditions we look to for our source material and inspiration appear over a span of dozens of centuries. Limiting ourselves to, say, the holdout traditions of the non-Christianized Irish of the 6th century would prevent us from looking to resources ranging from Caesar's *De Bello Gallico* to modern folk rituals at healing wells. We are developing a polytheistic Celtic tradition as it might have looked if left mostly to its own devices over the centuries, not a museum-ready replica of a bygone age.

Do I have to live in the country to be a CR?

Absolutely not.

Though reverence for nature is a core part of Celtic tradition, and many CRs prefer to live in rural areas, most are currently living in more urban environments. There are aspects of CR that are easier if one is living out in nature – it's easier to communicate with local nature spirits and form a deep bond with the land if these things are right outside one's front door. Some CRs feel raising their own food, for instance, is an integral part of their spirituality. But urban CRs are more likely to have access to libraries, language classes, and Celtic cultural events. They are also more likely to have a number of other CRs with whom to work and socialize. Urban CRs do still make connection with nature a part of their practice by familiarizing themselves with their local parks, arboretums and nature preserves, respecting the wildlife and flora that share their urban environment, cultivating a bond with the city's land and its natural features, and making regular pilgrimages to more wild settings when possible.

Ideally, in a region with both urban and rural CRs, community members help each other out – with rural CRs providing the land for ritual retreats out in nature, and urban CRs hosting guests for cultural events in the city. In this way, the diversity of the community results in a fuller experience for all members.

Do you work in groups or are you solitary?

Both. At the moment, there are very few groups that are larger than a hearth or household, but that's because there aren't a lot of CRs out there. Larger groups tend to get together for the major festivals, for feasting and making offerings to the Deities, ancestors and land spirits. These large, celebratory groups may also include visitors who aren't CR at all. Many of us practice by ourselves out of necessity, at least most of the time. But with increased visibility and networking on the Internet, more groups are developing as people meet in local areas, and as they discover others who are dedicated to the same Deities or are working on the same paths.

What do you call your groups?

As with so many other things on the CR path, this depends greatly on the group and its goals, as well as its cultural focus.

A family-based group might call themselves a Household or Hearth (or an equivalent in a Celtic language, such as *líon tí*), and may also include friends as part of their extended "family." A group devoted to study and scholarship might refer to itself as a

Hedge School or Druidic College. Those who meet mostly for purposes of worship might refer to their group as a Grove, *Nemeton, Nemed* ("temple, sanctuary," modern Irish *Naomheadh*) or *Fidnemed* ("woodland sanctuary," modern Irish *Fiodh-naomheadh*). Groups focused on their dedication to a particular Deity or cultural path may identify as Brighid orders or *fianna*-inspired warbands. Other groups may be loose, non-hierarchical collectives, who may identify as "Outsiders" or feel no need for a permanent, public name.

Some larger groups might consider calling themselves a *clann* ("extended family") or a *túath* ("tribe or nation, and the land the tribe/nation inhabits"). However, more traditional CRs see this as inappropriate; any modern, polytheistic groups currently using these terms have radically redefined them. Historically, and in the living cultures, these terms imply **huge** groups: either those who share a common, distant ancestor (such as the Highland *clann* organizations), or a large, land-based community of thousands of people. Even a "household" in ancient Irish terms was very sizeable - reckoned at about thirty people per dwelling. A *tríca cét* was roughly three thousand people, and a *túath* consisted of several allied *tríca céta*. Therefore, a *túath* only really applies to groups larger than six thousand people. In a modern sense, a *clann* would more accurately describe a huge, extended family of origin, such as one's birth family and relatives, all the way out to the very distant cousins (again, as seen in the Highland *clanns*). *Túath* would more aptly describe a town or small city.

Currently, there are no large, organized CR groups of that size, and though many of us include members of our families of origin in our celebrations, rituals and cultural events, there are no modern, Celtic polytheistic groups who fit the historical definition of a *clann* or *túath*.

The names of groups and any officiants in them will also be influenced by the cultures and languages that inspire them. Names of groups based on Welsh or Gaulish traditions will be different than those based in the Gaelic traditions of Ireland or Scotland. Though there is a respect for historical as well as contemporary context in our naming conventions, there are no hard and fast rules.

Do CRs have a distinction between clergy and laypeople?

Yes and no. In terms of household worship, we do not need external or intermediary clergy – each CR acts as their own conduit to spirituality, making offerings at our altars or outdoor shrines and connecting with the Deities, ancestors and nature spirits as we can. Sometimes the head of a household, or the member of the household with the most aptitude towards the work, will lead these sorts of rituals for their friends and family. In cases where a number of group members are experienced and skilled, these groups might work more collectively, sharing the leadership among all group members who are able to fulfill a role.

Within the larger community there are those who write and perform rituals for large groups at festivals or for holy days. Some among us are better at divination or healing, while others tend to things like weddings and child blessings. Others are good at teaching the basics of CR to others, while still other folk specialize in the philosophies and theologies of CR. Those folk who engage in the research and philosophy, in public ritual and healing, or in divinatory service to the community could be considered clergy, while those who prefer to act only within their own households tend to fall more into the laity category. At this point in CR's growth, there is no hard and fast distinction and most of us act as clergy at one point or another, if for no other reason than necessity.

Are CRs autonomous or is there some sort of governing body?

There is a good deal of autonomy in CR, and we do not have any official governing body. However, those who have been working together for the past fifteen to twenty-plus years to develop the CR tradition and community do tend to stay in touch with each other and keep an eye on how the tradition is developing. We have a lot of communication between groups and individuals, both old and new, in keeping with the Celtic values of respect and hospitality. We share with each other online and in person, and work through our UPG together to come up with patterns that fit across the spectrum. While no one speaks for CR as a whole, we do very much rely on the opinions of other CRs

The CR FAQ

when discussing the traditions publicly. That said, CR organizations may have their own governing bodies that deal with individuals within those organizations.

See also

✧ Who's the leader of CR? (p. 21)
✧ How do you determine who your spiritual elders are when you don't always have an ordered hierarchy? (p. 36)
✧ What is this UPG thing I keep hearing about? (p. 48)

How do you determine who your spiritual elders are when you don't always have an ordered hierarchy?

We look at what the individuals in question are doing for the community, what they're producing, and the results their works bring to the community.

Do they comport themselves with honor? Are they honest, ethical people? What do their students and/or their teachers say about them? What do others who have met them in person or interacted with them for a long time online have to say about them? What kinds of things are they teaching, and how closely does it seem to follow historical Celtic spiritual precedent? Do they bring valuable insight to discussions, set an example to emulate by their admirable behaviour, and produce scholarly, respected, and inspired work? Do they help to productively foster a feeling of community and the spiritual development of the individuals within it? Do their inspirations seem to work for a variety of people across the CR spectrum?

In traditional, land-based communities, no one was (or is) able to operate with the current anonymity provided by the Internet or the occasional festival gathering of strangers. You would know who someone's grandparents, parents and older siblings were. You would know the values held, and patterns of behaviour exhibited by, their family. They could not escape their own reputation.

In our modern world, we have to find ways to make up for this lack of long acquaintance. In CR, we cannot judge anyone by any titles they take for themselves. Rather, we learn about people by watching what they do. We must be patient and see how someone behaves in community over the long haul. Part of being an elder is actual physical age, as well as the wisdom and experience gained

36

by many years of participation in the tradition. Titles are not easily granted, nor can they be bought or self-proclaimed. They are earned. They result from community recognition, not individual self-aggrandizement or ego. Folks we consider elders are those who have had a positive impact on our practice and who have advanced CR as a whole through their teaching and their work.

Are there any CR organizations? Websites? Books?

There are a number of CR organizations, but none speak for the whole of the CR movement. There are also a number of websites where one may find CR writing and resources. Some of these represent organizations and online communities, but most are by individual CRs or household-size groups.

The CR FAQ is the first introductory book published that is wholly about CR. Previous to this publication, there was only one book that most CRs agree is about CR practices (Erynn Rowan Laurie's *Circle of Stones*). Over the next few years a variety of CR books will be published, and those new to the community will have an easier time getting up to speed. Right now, we have the same materials all CRs have relied upon to date: the old tales and manuscripts, the books of folkloric practices, and the collective wisdom of the community.

Online communities and discussion groups vary in quality and openness depending on the members of those lists and communities. When joining these communities, be prepared to offer sources to support your comments when asked, and remember that a question is not a challenge to you as a person, but merely a request for information.

Below are some CR email lists, communities, and discussion groups but we recommend checking the online version of this FAQ at *http://www.paganachd.com/faq* for fresh/current linkage goodness.

Discussion Groups

LiveJournal Celtic Reconstructionist/Restorationist community –
   http://community.livejournal.com/cr_r/
LiveJournal Pàganachd/Págánacht community –
   http://community.livejournal.com/paganacht/
Chicago Area CRs – *http://community.livejournal.com/chicagocelts/*

CRs in the Northeastern US and Canada –
   http://community.livejournal.com/ne_cr/
CRs in the US Plains region –
   http://community.livejournal.com/cr_prairie/
Puget Sound region –
   http://community.livejournal.com/puget_sound_crs/
Southeastern US –
   http://community.livejournal.com/southeastern_cr/
Southwestern US –
   http://community.livejournal.com/southwestern_cr/
The Imbas email list – *http://groups.yahoo.com/group/imbas-public/*
The Multicultural Polytheistic Hearth board –
   http://www.cyberpict.net/mph/
The Nemeton email list – *http://technovate.org/web/nemeton/*

Other Resources
CAORANN – *http://www.bandia.net/caorann/* – Celts Against
   Oppression, Racism and Neo-Nazism
Imbas website – *http://www.imbas.org/imbas/index.html/* – archive
   of articles
Pàganachd / Págánacht – *http://www.paganachd.com/* – "A Celtic
   Reconstructionist Gateway." Articles, resources, message
   board, and home of the online version of The CR FAQ

Contributor's Websites
bandia.net – *http://www.bandia.net/*
Dùn Sgàthan – *http://www.cyberpict.net/*
The Preserving Shrine – *http://www.seanet.com/~inisglas/*

What do CRs eat?

The official cuisine of CR is Indian Food. No one knows why.

In all seriousness, while there are no pan-CR food taboos, there are many individuals who use food choices and behaviours to deepen their spiritual connection to CR. There is a strong tradition of feasting as both celebration and offering of hospitality, and traditions which demand that a guest must be offered food, drink, and the chance to wash upon arrival. Many CRs extend this to a modern context, and will offer such hospitality to their guests.

Specific foods may be deliberately eaten or avoided to evoke spiritual effect. Some CRs will choose to consume salmon and/or hazelnuts as an effort to take wisdom into themselves, beef as a way to appreciate wealth and bounty, or pork to evoke feasting, plenty, and a possible connection with the Otherworld. Many will deliberately seek out locally-grown and produced food and consume it mindfully to commune with their local land spirits. Some Celtic Deities have specific food associations, such as Bríde's well-known association with milk and dairy products. This known association may be drawn upon in ritual, sharing a cup of milk or offering one. In the Irish materials, Manannán mac Lír and Goibhniu were involved in presenting the Feast of Age that gave immortality to the Túatha Dé Danann. The rite involved the sacrifice of a boar that returned to life the next day, and consuming ale brewed by Goibhniu. Some CRs hold feasts in commemoration of this involving pork and ale or mead.

In addition, individuals may have personal behavioural requirements called *geasa*, the breaching of which was a serious error often leading to one's downfall. Many of these relate to food. The ancient Irish hero Fergus was never allowed to refuse to attend a feast in his honor, and Cú Chulainn was prohibited from eating the meat of dogs while at the same time unable to refuse food offered by a woman. Some CRs believe that they have similar *geasa*, and will avoid foods that are personally proscribed.

Chapter Three

Intermediate Questions

What is the Celtic lore, and where can I find it?

When we refer to "the Celtic lore," we mean the collections of ancient manuscripts, the folklore gathered from the Celtic lands, and the many traditional tales, poems and songs.

There are differences in the level of accuracy and authenticity of the materials available. To get technical for a moment, material is generally characterized as one of the following: primary, secondary, and tertiary.

Primary source materials are the actual documents in the original language, usually found in museums, specialized libraries, and curated collections. These documents are often referred to as manuscripts, or MSS for short. Also considered primary material is folklore that was recorded exactly from the living sources, during the time these practices were still part of the living tradition, without being filtered through the interpretation of the interviewer.

Human error and human bias is always a factor to bear in mind, even with primary sources. Part of utilizing any source is to understand the context in which the information was recorded, and to take into account any possible biases on the part of the recorder, whether that recorder was a Christian monk or someone's great-grandmother. One of the ways we strive for accuracy is to compare all the different records of lore and practices, and through these comparisons a fuller, more accurate picture usually emerges.

Secondary material is the primary material in translation, along with what is written by those examining these documents, doing research and drawing conclusions. To do this sort of work takes some skill and training in the proper methodologies. Skilled amateurs may be able to do this sort of work, but because of the lack of peer review, their conclusions may not be valid.

CRs generally consider tertiary research unreliable. Tertiary research does not look at primary sources at all. It only looks at secondary sources of varying quality and draws conclusions from that material. The further away from the source documents and evidence you get, the less certain you can be of the conclusions.

There are also various compiled manuscript bodies called editions, in which a scholar has compared several manuscripts claiming to tell the same story, closely examined all the evidence, and selected what they believe to be the single most coherent and likely version of the original. Due to the editorial nature of the process, there is some uncertainty and potential bias introduced when this occurs, and there will be differences between manuscript editions produced by different scholars. This process is usually only attempted by accomplished and erudite scholars after many years of study, due to the high level of background knowledge that good compilation requires. Many CRs will study different editions of ancient manuscript texts in an effort to gain a fuller and deeper understanding of the source material.

See also

✧ The Ever-Popular Reading List Section (p. 145)

Do you have to speak a Celtic language (Gaelic, Welsh, etc.) to be CR? How important is language? Are you all fluent in a Celtic language?

It's not necessary to speak a Celtic language fluently to be CR. We do encourage people to understand particular words in the Celtic languages that are, so to speak, the technical vocabulary of CR, and to immerse themselves as much as they are able in the language of the culture on which they are focused. The Welsh have said "no country without a language," and we tend to agree with this philosophy. Unless we understand something of how different languages work, we can't understand the worldviews of the people who speak them, and Celtic languages present a different worldview than English or German or Russian.

For some of us, learning and speaking a language is a more personal and profound project. It can be important to offer at least a few words in prayer in a Celtic language, particularly if one of your Deities has requested this of you. Some of us even began our study of a Celtic language after dreams or visions in which we believe a Deity asked us to speak to Them in the language, or spoke to us in that language, and we set out on a quest to see what They were asking of us. A number of us learn songs and poetry in Celtic languages as a way to help preserve the cultures we're working within – or just because it's fun and exciting – in much the same way that we might study Irish dance or Scottish piping.

It is also useful to note that even though the Deities may understand English perfectly well, it is the language of those who oppressed many of Their people. It may not always be the best idea to address one's Deities in the language that accompanied cultural genocide.

It's also important to realize that some concepts can't be easily or completely translated from a Celtic language into English, and so for a proper grasp of the idea, learning to think in the language becomes important. If you're just starting in CR, nobody is going to make you learn an entire ritual liturgy in a foreign language. Though many of us have fluency as a goal, most of us aren't actually fluent, even if we've been studying Celtic languages for years.

What's the difference between a warrior path and a poet's path? Are there other options within CR?

People come to CR for many reasons. Some feel a pull toward the more mystical side, while others feel called to public service of Deity and community. Some people feel called to follow warrior Deities, while others are interested in the Deities of the arts and crafts. Those who are dedicated to Deities of making might study metalsmithing and jewelry, weaving, or woodworking.

There is a place for each type of person and for those who are interested in more than one of these paths. Historically, some people were both warriors and poets, or druids and artists. Sometimes mastery of one path included study of another, such as the requirement for members of Finn's warrior *fianna* to be able to memorize, compose, and present poems. The arts of the warrior required physical discipline like that of Asian martial artists, and could take a lifetime to master, just as the arts of the druid do. What all of us have in common is a dedication to Celtic cultures and Deities, with a love of Celtic music, arts, and languages. Any well-rounded living culture will have a place for many diverse kinds of people and their different talents and abilities, and it is this diversity that CR fosters.

People may study warrior arts for self-defense, for self-discipline, or to understand themselves more deeply. Some of those who embrace the warrior path bring this into their lives through working in law enforcement, fire fighting and rescue, emergency medical services, search and rescue, or military service. Those called to a poetic path might be more interested in ecstatic states and traversing the mysteries of the mists between the worlds to bring back knowledge for the community. People on the druid's path create ritual and study history and the tales to be able to share them with others, providing continuity within the CR community. Those who are more involved with their own home and hearth participate through keeping personal altars and honoring the ancestors and the land spirits of the place where they live and by hosting feasts in their homes on holy days. And while specialization and focus can be very important, especially in a time when we are working to flesh out a number of these traditions, many will find themselves drawn to creating a unique path that combines aspects of a number of these approaches.

See also

✧ You talk a lot about the role of the Outsiders. What do you mean by that? (p. 91)

I've read about Cú Chulainn's training with Scáthach. What is this "Salmon Leap" or the "sword feat"? Is there a Celtic Martial Art form?

As far as we know, there was never a single, unitary Celtic martial art form, but there were a number of techniques used in training for martial activity.

A variety of martial sports still exist in the Celtic lands which are fairly certainly derived from early Celtic combative techniques. These include some forms of "fixed-hold" wrestling, such as the Irish "Collar-and-Elbow" wrestling, Scottish Backhold, Breton Gouren, and Cornish Wrestling. The "Catch as Catch Can" style of wrestling, which eventually branched into the pure entertainment of "Professional Wrestling," as well as the combative submission fighting of Catch Wrestling, derives from northern Welsh and Lancashire wrestling. Even the minor sport of Shin Kicking (also known as "Purring") develops from fixed-hold wrestling of the sort called "Out-Play" (as opposed to "In-Play"). There are a number of fixed-hold wrestling styles from around the world, so the simple presence of a fixed-hold wrestling style does not necessarily indicate Celtic antecedents. The history must be examined carefully.

Boxing owes much (though not, by any means, all) of its history to fistfighting techniques in the Celtic lands, notably Ireland. Many of the earliest professional boxers were from Ireland, both in Europe and later in America.

Additionally, there are a few weapon styles which have survived, at least in instruction manuals. Methods of fencing with the broadsword or the "shillelagh" (*bata* or stick), as well as other weapons, exist both in direct transmission and in detailed description in books.

The "Salmon Leap" is one of the *cleasa* ("Feats" or "Tricks") said to have been known by Cú Chulainn prior to arriving on the Isle of Skye, where he traveled to pursue training with Scáthach (a renowned teacher of martial arts, said to have a school on Skye). He makes use of the leap in his "audition," as it were, to her for instruction. It is also one of the most commonly reported "Feats" of the Irish heroes, though there were other impressive *cleasa* as well. Classical commentators, in discussing their battles against the Gauls, noted that the Celtic peoples would leap over the shields of their opponents. The "Salmon Leap," it seems, was simply learning high jumping techniques and practicing them until the warrior could jump up in the air higher than most.

The "Sword Feat" (*Faobhar Chleas*) is described in some detail in the story *Mesca Ulad* ("The Intoxication of the Ulstermen"). It consisted of a dance engaged in prior to combat, involving juggling the sword and other impressive moves. It's likely that a number of other "feats" listed as known by Cú Chulainn were similar in nature (such as the "Body Feat," which may have been a dance which demonstrated unarmed combat techniques).

Celtic warriors did not, apparently, stop at simply learning how to hit someone with a weapon. They also engaged in practices which today we might call "cross-training," and in methods which were more clearly "magical" in nature.

For a much more detailed article on this subject, see "**Celtic Martial Arts**"[3] by C. Lee Vermeers.

Can women be warriors too?

The existence of women warriors in Celtic cultures is highly debated. Although many CRs and scholars believe there is evidence, we must note that the evidence is circumstantial and arguable at this time. Until a clearly identified Celtic woman's body is discovered buried with weapons, this is the best we have to work with. Whether or not there were professional women warriors among the Celtic ancestors, there is definitely a place for women warriors in CR, as we are not recreating the past.

As the ancient Celts were a warrior culture, our modern ideas of who is and isn't a warrior may not be applicable to the way the Celtic ancestors lived. Women were, and are, expected to be willing and able to fight, especially at times of extreme crisis. This is something we know from historical times. For example, although it would not have been considered appropriate for Scottish women of the late 18th century to become soldiers, when the need arose during the Highland Clearances many women did take up the battle physically. Women were also known to join in the Irish Faction Fights, which could be anything from mild skirmishes to full-out, bloody battles. While it is unclear to what extent *professional* women warriors were common at any time in Celtic history, it is clear that Celtic women were prepared to fight – whether in defense of themselves, their people or their territory.

There are instances of early Celtic women who fought and led armies in battle, as attested by the Romans. The most famous of these is Boudicca, queen of the British Iceni, who led a multi-tribal rebellion against the Romans after her husband's death, the rape of her daughters and her own flogging in the first century C.E.

---

[3] *http://www.paganachd.com/articles/celticmartialarts.html*

This was recorded by the Roman historians Dio Cassius and Tacitus. It is often noted that there is no evidence that she had actual training in arms or that women were amongst her warriors; however, it should be noted that if the mind set of a warrior people does not include women as capable warriors the men are not likely to follow one into battle. Ammianus and Diodorus Siculus both described Gaulish women as being as large as the men and indicated that they were better fighters than their men. Tacitus as well as Caesar remarked on women at least being present to cheer the warriors on, and who were often killed or wounded in battle, although they do not mention women actually fighting; Plutarch, on the other hand, noted Gaulish women staying behind the battle lines to kill their own men if they retreated.

Based on new evidence, some of us are considering that we may now have to rethink our belief that the Romans would have noted women warriors in the battle field. Perhaps the women who are often seen as "just cheerleaders" were remarkable in that, despite their presence on the field of battle, they were *not* fighting. It's possible the Romans simply did not note the women who might have fought. In 2004, the discovery of graves at a Roman fort in Cumbria included several women burned and buried with horses and weapons, indicating that the Romans themselves had female mercenaries (Sarmatians?) among their troops. There is no written record of these women so, if we now have this hard evidence and they didn't bother mentioning it, would they mention women fighting among their enemies as being odd? However, we do not yet have any reports of Celtic women warrior's graves.

The mythology contains a number of references to Goddesses of war and slaughter. In some of these tales the Goddesses, or what may have been priestesses of these Goddesses, are seen on the battlefield spurring the warriors on, or depicted in animal form joining the battle. Actual accounts of Goddesses and women who took up arms and ruled by right of conquest are less common, but they do exist even if some are debated. For instance, in the *Cath Maige Tuired* when the Morrígan exclaims that She will kill as Her contribution to the battle, many choose to interpret this as by magic even though it's never stated if She will act by arms or magic. More clear is the story of Macha the Red, who ruled by right of conquest, having defeated a series of other claimants to the throne (all men) in battle. Medb and Carman led armies into battle, much as Queen Boudicca did historically. The woman warrior Scáthach trained Cú Chulainn, and he was challenged to a fight by the neighboring warrior woman Aoife, whom he defeated only by cheating. Fionn Mac Cumhail was also fostered by a woman or women who taught him to fight. It is among the Outsiders, the *fianna*, that we see many accounts of women warriors, including Ness who led a *fianna* band for a period of time and Creidne, who, after her father raped her and she bore three sons, went Outlaw until she won inheritance right for her sons. As often is the case, even if women warriors are not welcome in mainstream culture, women drawn to the path find roles Outside of it.

This attitude has survived to some extent into modern times, in that many women who are descended from these fierce ancestors were raised with the attitude that, when called for, we must be willing and able to fight. In this spirit, CR women often study martial arts and some work in professions that could be considered modern expressions of the warrior path.

See also
- ✧ What's the difference between a warrior path and a poet's path? (p. 43)
- ✧ You talk a lot about the role of the Outsiders. What do you mean by that? (p. 91)
- ✧ Why would anyone want to try to bring back the Iron Age? (p. 69)

What is this UPG thing I keep hearing about?

UPG = Unsubstantiated Personal Gnosis. This is a label used to identify information gained through meditation, intense flashes of intuition, visions, and other spiritual experiences. Often this information may not be verifiable through primary or academic sources but seems to be usable in personal ways. CRs consider it highly important to label UPG which cannot be substantiated by lore or research as such, as this helps prevent misunderstandings about verifiable sources and preserves intellectual honesty. "UPG" and its variants are used specifically to indicate beliefs arrived at via *mystical* means, not ideas or intellectual conclusions reached from academic research.

Variant phrasings of UPG are Unverified or Undocumented Personal Gnosis.

Though it is unclear exactly who first coined the term UPG, consensus holds that the term and its variants originated in the Ásatrú communities some time in the 1990s. These terms have been gratefully adopted by many Reconstructionist traditions and further refined and applied in our communities.

Related terms:

SPG (Shared Personal Gnosis) - indicating a mystical vision and belief shared by a number of people; preferably, one arrived at independently of one another and arising from people who are otherwise unconnected. For instance, a vision experienced collectively by the members of a small household may have more validity to it than a vision by a sole individual but, due to the possibility of group hallucination, it is debatable whether this small-group gnosis truly qualifies as SPG. A vision experienced by geographically separated people who have never met one another is more in tune with what we consider SPG.

CG (Confirmed Gnosis) - indicating that substantiating evidence for an incidence of UPG or SPG has later been found in the lore. This is also sometimes referred to as CPG (Confirmed Personal Gnosis). These instances are highly valued, and have served to bolster individual and community faith in the Deities, spirits or ancestors from whom the information was received. Instances of CG are also very important in that over time they help us learn to distinguish true *imbas* from imagination. (*Imbas* is the Old Irish word for "inspiration." In Modern Irish it is spelled *iomas*.)

UPG is never an end in and of itself; rather, it is the beginning of a journey, the beginning of the process of testing the information through both spiritual practice and academic research. UPG is only useful when the community also values humility and fact-checking, and acknowledges that even the most experienced mystic can at times become deluded or make mistakes. At some point or another we have *all* had to discard some cool dream or "vision" if it simply does not line up with the lore, or if it threatened to take us in a direction that was counter to our values. Similarly, though we have some people who have shown skill in mediating for the Deities and spirits, and for bringing back information from the Otherworlds, we have no desire to take the dangerous step of setting up anyone as an infallible guru or voice of the Divine.

When considering whether someone's UPG or SPG may be worthy of inclusion in your spiritual practice, these *"Laws of UPG"*[4] may serve as a useful guide:

1. No UPG should contradict known facts about the associated culture, and no practices based only on UPG should stand as more than modern inventions.
2. If a belief or practice based on UPG does not contradict known facts, but cannot be verified within the same body of knowledge, it remains a modern invention.
3. If an instance of UPG fits rule 2 and also fills a gap in known tradition, it is probably worth pursuing further, through experimentation and research, to see if it can become SPG or CG.
4. If an instance of UPG that meets the second law is arrived at by people who have had no real contact with each other, it remains modern but is Shared (SPG). This means the group just may be getting somewhere interesting.
5. If an instance of UPG becomes SPG, and said SPG is then incorporated into the practices of those outside of the groups who first experienced it, it becomes a modern tradition.
6. There is no way for UPG to become ancient lore unless it becomes generally accepted and then is kept mostly intact for at least 1,000 years.

How much UPG is acceptable in CR? How do you know?

CR, like all traditions with a mystical, ecstatic side, needs to have checks and balances in order to remain healthy. Those who work with trance states, journeying, and other forms of interacting with Deities and spirits, need to have a solid support system that they can turn to for feedback, grounded discussion of similar or shared experiences, and reality checks against the known Celtic lore and cultural knowledge.

While CRs living all over the world have sometimes experienced unpredictable things, such as local spirits appearing in a Celtic guise, or spirits who claim to be Celtic Deities appearing

---

[4] *http://branruadh.blogspot.com/2006/02/laws-of-upg.html*

in unusual forms or with unusual messages, every mystic worth their salt knows that these things have to be tested against the lore and the perceptions of other mystics before they take them as anything more than imagination. It is not uncommon for our minds to create projections of our expectations. If you find yourself dealing with an entity that's offering you the wisdom of the universe, chances are very good that it's your mind you've met, and not a spirit or Deity.

It's very important to consult with other mystics, visionaries, seers, and lore-keepers about the information that you receive in your trance and ecstatic work. This is also why our reading in the traditional lore and texts is so important – it allows us to compare new information against a known cultural matrix to see if it *fits*. It also helps to bear in mind that just because the Ancestors are dead doesn't mean that they're any wiser than they were in life. Always test answers and information you gain from spiritual work against common sense and the known facts. It's well known that some of the Deities are tricksters as well, and while we may respect Them, we cannot always trust Them completely. It is vital to examine everything you learn before using it in ritual or bringing it to the community as anything other than your own UPG.

Remember also that the agendas of the spirits and the Deities are not necessarily our own. If they ask you for something you cannot reasonably provide, tell them so and explain why. Be extremely cautious if you receive messages of any sort that suggest you harm yourself or others. Not everyone in the Otherworlds has your best interests at heart.

When approached cautiously, with a firm support network and a good grounding in tradition and lore, UPG can be a very useful part of CR practice. Some UPG eventually becomes accepted within CR as a whole as valid and valuable group practice as well as being useful to the individual receiving the insight. Remember that all of us have to throw out lovely ideas from time to time because there's contradictory evidence in the lore and traditions or because facts stand against it. In those cases, such insights may be useful in personal practice, but don't have a place in CR as a whole.

See also

✧ What is this UPG thing I keep hearing about? (p. 48)

✧ What is the Celtic lore, and where can I find it? (p. 41)

In regards to relating to a Deity, how much should one be in concordance with the myths? With history?

See

✧ How much UPG is acceptable in CR? How do you know? (p. 50)

✧ That's not how my (*insert family member here*) taught me to honor (*insert figure of choice here*)! (p. 62)

How do you decide what aspects of Celtic culture to keep and what to discard?

Since the basic purpose of CR is to reconstruct what Celtic Pagan religions could have become in the modern age, we must, with great respect for the ancient and living traditions, adapt ancient spiritual practices to fit within modern society's legal and ethical structures. In other words, it's more dishonorable to break socially just laws of the country we live in than it would be for us to set aside those practices which are now illegal, ethically inappropriate, or impractical to the point of impossibility in a modern context. Carrying home the severed heads of worthy enemies is a poor idea for modern CR practice.

Iron Age tribal social structures are an impracticality that we have laid aside. CR has no High Kings, no Tribal Chieftains. There are not enough of us to qualify as actual CR nations or *túatha* (a *túath* was actually thousands of people – the size of a town or small city), and those are political titles that are inappropriate for a spiritual-social community living within the laws of the sovereign nations where we reside. It is also offensive to the living Celtic cultures to attempt to radically redefine what these terms and titles already mean, and as we are involved in the living Celtic cultures, it would not even occur to us to do something so offensive. While we may strive toward the better ideals of tribalism, community and collectivism, we do not believe it is our place to claim a region of the country as our "territory" and attempt (or pretend) to rule over it in any way. It is our desire instead to interact with the spirits of the land, the ancestors and the Deities in a respectful way, and to coexist peacefully and constructively with our human neighbors, no matter their background or religion.

We encourage people to contemplate what is good and useful about early Celtic cultures. We all attempt to cultivate a personal and communal sense of Celtic virtues such as Truth, Honor, Justice, Loyalty, Courage, Community, Hospitality, Strength, and Gentleness and to implement these values in our modern lives in ways that work for us. For some, this leads to community service in either a personal or a professional capacity. Others find in it a call to political activism for peace and justice. Some of us simply find it a way to help us live our lives as better, more compassionate individuals.

Do you borrow from other cultures to "fill in the gaps"?

Borrow? No. Steal? One certainly hopes not. Use broad as well as deep study, especially of closely-related cultures, to help form a working hypothesis of how the Celtic ancestors may have done something? Yes, sometimes.

When we speak of studying other related cultures for ideas on how to elaborate on some of the Celtic religious practices for which we have scant information, we are not advocating simply importing rituals, practices or beliefs from other traditions. Often, we are only going as far afield as looking at Welsh or Gaulish lore for hints to the missing pieces in the Gaelic. Others may look at the common elements found in a number of other Indo-European cultures for signposts for what we may be missing, especially to the Norse, which has historically interacted rather extensively with Celtic cultures in both the Islands and on the Continent.

However, many CRs are fine on keeping the tradition simple, sticking with the practices we have, and not attempting to elaborate anything.

CR was developed to provide an alternative to those "Celtic religions" that were really just putting knotwork on ways foreign to the Celtic cultures (namely Wicca, generic Neopaganism and "core shamanism") and that were pillaging Celtic cultures for a few exotic bits to spice up an otherwise eclectic practice. Therefore, a key element of CR is the deliberate avoidance of mixing our practice with other cultural practices. If we must "fill in the gaps," we would be more likely to use ideas from other Celtic cultures, or at least other Indo-European cultures, to help us develop something Celtic to fill the gap. It is crucial to understand that instead of just forcing foreign practices into a Celtic framework, we use them as "hints" – "okay, this was done in an ancient Norse ceremony, and it bears a strong resemblance to this ceremony found in a Vedic text, and here's a reference in this Irish text... oh, wait, maybe a similar thing was done among the Celts but it would have been more like this instead."

In doing reconstruction work, it is vitally important to first have a thorough grounding in the particular Celtic culture whose practices we are reconstructing. Without that, it is too easy for people to try to bring in things that are not only disharmonious with Celtic culture, but even for them to unknowingly try to unnecessarily replace things for which we already have working, Celtic examples. This is another area in which Celtic Reconstruction requires patience and years of study. Thankfully, as the movement matures, the years of study are being somewhat distilled so new folks don't have to continually re-invent the wheel, as it were. But they must also understand that even those of us who've been doing this for many years are still making sure all of our wheels work.

When sufficient hints cannot be found in closely-related cultures, some feel that it is appropriate to look further afield to other tribal and animistic cultures, such as the Afro-Diasporic traditions, in order to flesh out the tradition. However, this is an area of some controversy in CR. Different individuals and CR sub-traditions sometimes have divergent opinions on how appropriate this is; but even among those who look to wide-ranging sources there is still agreement that this is only for hints to how to do something in a Celtic way. It is a quest for adaptable "technologies" and not for replacement beliefs. One example of this would be the "exchange student" approach some have undertaken to learn how to safely manage ecstatic trance techniques. This began separately among several unrelated members of the CR community because these things were already happening sometimes in Celtic ceremonies. Our Deities seemed to be demanding that at least some of us perform this trance function, so this necessitated looking to experienced elders of living traditions for advice on how to safely ride out these experiences. Rather than deny the Celtic Deities, we wanted to find a way to safely deepen our connection and communication with Them – not only for ourselves, but also in service to the larger community. But among those who have been deeply affected by cross-cultural studies, and who are on speaking terms with Deities of other cultures, there is still the shared principle that as we develop our various CR traditions, non-Celtic practices should not be imported whole cloth. We want a vibrant and deep *Celtic* tradition, not an eclectic one.

Does CR include syncretisms?

In considering this question, it is crucial to recognize the difference between ancient syncretisms and recent ones, as well as the differences between syncretism and eclecticism.

Ancient syncretisms, which reflect longstanding parts of the living Celtic cultures and their historical interactions with other cultures, may be acceptable within a CR practice. However, syncretisms which are recent impositions of foreign ideas are not seen as CR.

While recent syncretisms are not accepted as part of CR, some CRs feel that **historical** syncretisms, which occurred as ancient polytheistic cultures interacted over a long period of time, have become a legitimate part of the living traditions. A common example of this is the presence of some Nordic customs and Deities found among the Scottish traditions, and the many other examples of the ways these cultures historically intermingled and influenced one another. These sorts of ancient, polytheistic syncretisms that grew out of lengthy cultural interaction are seen as different from the syncretisms of oppression which were instituted with the aim of co-opting and eventually eclipsing the native religions.

Eclecticism involves the combination of diverse beliefs and practices from a variety of unrelated cultures. The only "authority" generally recognized by eclectics is their own sense of "what feels right." Syncretism is somewhat different. Syncretism involves a main culture that one is rooted in, but which also incorporates some elements from an outside culture that seem to be harmonious with the syncretist's main cultural focus.

Eclecticism is absolutely not part of CR. Recent syncretisms are not accepted as CR.

The only syncretisms that most CR elders seem to agree are acceptable are those which have become a longstanding part of the living Celtic cultures, due to long-term cross-pollination. This includes the cross-pollination with Norse culture, some aspects of Celtic Christianity, and the overlap between related Celtic cultures such as the Gaelic and Gaulish.

There are some CRs who are doing cross-cultural studies, or who have backgrounds in a variety of cultural approaches to religion. However, CRs agree that such studies are meant to help form a better understanding of Celtic cultures in context, rather than to confuse or dilute the Celtic cultural focus of CR.

Can I be CR and still worship non-Celtic Deities?

Yes, but with caveats.

Worshipping non-Celtic Deities is regarded as outside the purview of CR, and should in no way be considered a part of CR practice. While it is acceptable for people involved in the CR community to have non-CR practices in their personal lives, it should be kept firmly in mind that they are just that – non-CR practices. The cultures and rites of non-Celtic Deities should be respected, just as we expect Celtic cultures and Deities to be respected, and these rites should be kept separate from your CR practice. If you worship Deities of other cultures, separate altars should be maintained for Them, and offerings and other rites should be undertaken in the ways of that Deity's culture.

If you feel a particular pull to Kali, for example, it is highly recommended that you worship Her through a local Hindu temple, or at least in traditional Hindu ways, rather than attempting to bring Kali into your CR practice. She is not a Celtic Goddess and would probably resent being treated as such. She already has Her own formulated and traditional rites and practices, Her own preferred offerings, and Her own holy days. To ignore those things in an attempt to fit Her into a CR practice would be doing violence to both CR and Hinduism.

The only times when it might be acceptable to worship non-Celtic Deities in a CR format would be in the cases where long-standing, historical interactions between related cultures created a hybrid cultural environment that traditionally included these Deities. For instance, in the cases of some Highland Scotland and coastal Irish communities that adopted some of the Norse Deities and customs. If the cultures had enough similarity, and it is clearly evident that these two cultures did meet and mingle and create an historical tradition, it is often considered acceptable to continue to include these long-standing syncretisms as part of that tradition.

See also

✧ Does CR include syncretisms? (p. 55)

What is this Ogham stuff you keep mentioning?

Ogham (or in Old Irish, *ogam*), pronounced "Ohm" or "OH-um," is the earliest form of a written Gaelic language – an alphabet and cipher originally devised under Latin influence. There are twenty *ogham feánna* (letters/glyphs), which are organized into four sets of five. Each set is an *aicme*. The first three *aicme* are made up of consonants and the fourth is made up of vowels. There is also a fifth *aicme* called the *forfeda* (extra letters) that are rarely, if ever, seen outside of manuscripts. The *forfeda* are definitely of later origin than the original character set. Whether they were the creation of the monks who wrote them down as an attempt to bring it in line with Latin or an independent development of a living system is a matter of some debate. Some CRs working with *ogham* as a divination system incorporate the *forfeda*, others do not.

Most *ogham* inscriptions which have survived are on large boundary stones, and simply give a name in the genitive case, often with a patronymic or matronymic or the name of an individual's grandfather. *Ogham* inscriptions are much like a Continental Celtic language in their morphology, and the Irish language changed more between the *Ogham* period to the Old Irish period (with about three centuries or so of crossover) than it has ever since.

In Old Irish narrative texts, *ogham* is often described as having been written on sticks of wood or wooden objects (like shields), but no such artifacts have survived. A few bone artifacts with individual letters, either dice or bones with possibly magical inscriptions, do survive. Use of *ogham* for divinatory purposes seems likely, given the attestation in the Second Vision of Adomnan that one of many diabolic arts that the Irish practiced was *fidlanna*, "divination by wood."

Many CRs use *ogham* for divination, sometimes through casting or drawing a *fiodh* (lit. "stick," usually used to indicate an *ogham* letter/glyph inscribed on a piece of wood), much like the

Norse use runes, and through studying the symbol systems as a way of interpreting omens in the world around us. CRs who use *ogham* for divination and meditation study the old texts and work with our inspiration and the feedback of other CRs to learn and further develop the system. This results in each letter becoming a point in an entire matrix of symbolic and conceptual associations. Many CRs look to the *Book of Ballymote* and its section on *ogham* alphabets and ciphers for historical associations and symbolism. However, particular approaches to the inclusion of *ogham* in a modern setting vary, with some CRs focusing on the tree associations for each letter and their ties to natural forces, others on the linguistic analysis of letter-name meanings or the word-association kennings and their poetic connection, and still others to the bird *ogham*, fortress *ogham*, color *ogham*, cipher *ogham*, or other historically attested ways of interpreting the *feánna*.

For one method of working with the *crann ogham* (tree *ogham*) from a CR perspective, see *"Treehuggers: A Methodology for Crann Ogham Work"*[5] by Raven nic Rhóisín and Kathryn Price NicDhàna.

Is it Samhain, Samhuinn or Samain? Why all these different spellings?

This can be a bit confusing to the learner, as we are sometimes discussing Old Irish sources, other times Scottish ones, other times other Celtic languages entirely. Just as modern English is different from the English spoken in Shakespeare's time, so have the Celtic languages evolved over time.

Therefore, spellings and pronunciations will vary depending on the specific Celtic language (Irish, Scottish, Welsh, Gaulish, etc), and the time period during which the material was recorded. As "Celtic Reconstructionism" has become an umbrella term, which encompasses many individuals and groups, of a variety of Celtic cultures and approaches, we see no need to force any standardization of these words. Usually, one will use the spellings/pronunciations that make most sense in context of a particular discussion, or those of the language which they know the best. For example, when explaining our tradition to someone from the broader, Neopagan community, we may use the most commonly understood name for a festival or Deity. But when

---

[5] *http://www.paganachd.com/articles/treehuggers.html*

referring to an ancient manuscript, we are more likely to stay true to the spellings used in that manuscript.

For the sake of introducing a bit of consistency to this FAQ, we have tended to standardize terms to Modern Irish. CR is a modern community, so some CRs feel strongly that we should use contemporary terminology, except in cases where no modern word exists for the concept we are trying to name. Also, Modern Irish is probably the most widespread of the Celtic languages, and therefore easier to find classes in than some of the others. This is in no way intended as a slight to those on Scottish, Welsh, Gaulish or other paths, but merely a way of making this document more understandable to those who speak none of the Celtic languages.

Here are some examples of different spellings used for the same terms and concepts. When more than one variation per language is given, the variations are listed from the oldest known form of the name to the spelling in current use. An asterisk (*) before a word indicates that it is a reconstructed form:

Festivals Approx. dates	Old Irish	Modern Irish (Gaeilge)	Scottish Gaelic (Gàidhlig)	Gaulish	Welsh (Cymraeg)
Beginning of November	Samain; Samhain	Oíche Shamhna	Samhuinn; Samhainn; Samhain	Samonios; *Trinouxtion Samonii	Calan Gaeaf
Beginning of February	Imbolc; Imbolg; Oimelc	Lá Fhéile Bríde; Imbolc	Là Fhèill Brìghde; Imbolc	*Ouiamelgtis	Gwyl Ffraed
Beginning of May	Beltain	Lá Bealtaine	Bealltuinn; Bealltainn	*Belotenia	Calan Mai
Beginning of August	Lughnasa; Lughnasad; Lughnassadh	Lá Lúnasa	Lùnasdal; Lùnastal	*Lugunassatis	Calan Awst

This all sounds like a lot of work. Why would anyone want to work that hard when they could just join an established religion?

Yes, at this stage in its development, CR does tend to be a lot of work. It's not for everyone.

Though we are at a place where people who don't want to do lots of research or pioneering mystical experiments can join an existing CR group, and participate on a much more informal level, the truth is that functioning CR groups that are willing to take in new members are still few and far between. So if you're alone, you may feel that it is difficult, especially if you are just getting started. Right now CR favors pioneer species, so to speak.

One of the main reasons we began this work was that we believe the Celtic Deities and Ancestors were, and are, asking it of us. Independent experiences by unrelated individuals have led to Shared Gnosis that several Deities in particular were eager to see CR happen. So a number of people sworn to these Deities found ourselves becoming very driven to create a functional, authentically Celtic tradition in order to better serve Them. A number of us were also inspired by our experiences in other living cultures and wished for something that full and vital, not only for our own Deities and Ancestors, but also for ourselves. It will be a while till we are as fleshed out as the traditions that inspired us, but that is our goal.

See also

✧ What is this UPG thing I keep hearing about? (p. 48)

Chapter Four

Misconceptions

Why are you racist?

CR is firmly anti-racist. This has been unanimously agreed upon by representatives of the established CR sub-traditions, CR elders and other long-term members of the community, including the founders of the tradition. CR was founded in no small part because some of us were sick of the rampant cultural appropriation in the Neopagan community, and wished to devote ourselves to something that was our own, that honored the ways of our ancestors without needing to rip off anyone else's ancestors or cultures in the process. There is no ethnic or cultural requirement for anyone to practice CR – we do not believe that "blood" has any bearing in spirituality or in who might be called to a particular path. And as Celtic identity is a matter of language and culture, "blood" really has nothing to do with whether or not an individual or tradition is Celtic. No matter where your ancestors were from, or what your ethnic background, you are welcome to practice CR with us.

See also

- ✧ What do you mean by "Celtic"? (p. 18)
- ✧ What makes your ancestors any better than *my* ancestors? (p. 62)
- ✧ Don't you have to be Irish/Scottish/Welsh to be a Celtic Reconstructionist? (p. 27)
- ✧ What is the ethical basis of CR? (p. 111)

Also *"The CR Essay"*[6] and CAORANN - *Celts Against Oppression, Racism and Neo-Nazism.*[7]

What makes your ancestors any better than *my* ancestors?

Nothing, and nobody who is actually practicing CR believes that the early Celts were inherently any "better" than anyone else. While many people of Celtic heritage are drawn to CR, and respecting our ancestors is important to us, no particular ethnicity or nationality has ever been a requirement. A significant number of people in CR don't have any physical ancestors from the Celtic lands, though they do participate in the living Celtic cultures and consider the Celtic peoples to be their spiritual ancestors. We follow Celtic Deities and explore Celtic traditions because we are drawn to them and what they have to say about the human condition and human spirituality. People practicing or endorsing racism are not accepted as a part of CR any more than KKK members are accepted as a part of mainstream liberal Christian denominations. We work hard to expose people using CR or a link with Celtic culture as an excuse for racism and condemn them for their prejudices and acts of discrimination.

See also

✦ What about this ancestor reverence and land spirit stuff? (p. 86)

That's not how my (*insert family member here*) taught me to honor (*insert figure of choice here*)!

As will happen in any living culture, some of the tales do exist in different versions. Similarly, folkloric practices and the meaning and use of various magical objects can vary a bit from region to region. However, as a whole, the Celtic oral traditions have been remarkably conservative. We have versions of tales recorded at the turn of the century that hardly vary at all from the same tale in ancient manuscripts. Given this inherent consistency, when someone appears in the community and puts forth a bizarre set of mythological associations and claims they

---

[6] *www.witchvox.com/trads/trad_cr.html*
[7] *http://www.bandia.net/caorann/*

are valid because they learned them that way from their family, it is understandable that these claims are greeted with skepticism.

Usually when a variant meaning is valid, some supporting evidence, such as other tales and folklore from the region, can be found. But in cases where these sorts of assertions clash radically with everything that is known of the region they claim to be from, yes, it's usually a case of someone making things up or having been taught by someone who made it up.

Don't you all just read books and argue rather than practice real spirituality?

Most of us are very spiritual people in our private lives. We have altars in our homes and do personal and family-centered devotional work. Some of us do divination or healing, or perform ritual services within our communities. Reading doesn't mean we're not spiritual. In fact, for most of us, the reading we do enhances our spirituality and helps us understand what we are taught by other people and what comes to us through more mystical means such as in visions, meditations or dreams. Reference books, written by those who have devoted their lives to studying the words and traditions of the ancestors, help us sort out what is traditionally Celtic from what is our own internal voice. Both may be valid, but our inner voice may not be entirely accurate about what is Celtic, or what is communication from the Divine and what is our own imaginations. When we believe we are receiving information from a Deity or spirit, we go to the scholars to compare notes and see what's Celtic and what's not.

The CR community is diverse. Not everyone is an experienced scholar, and not everyone is inclined to deep mystical work. However, we believe both scholarship and experiential, ecstatic spirituality are necessary on the CR path. The presence of, and balance between, these aspects is crucial. Without both, it is not CR. But people will tend to move towards what is more comfortable and desirable for them. Sometimes the balance has to be found in community, where the mystics and the scholars can work together to help inform one another's practices. In this way, we can co-create a vibrant tradition that honors our personal experiences as well as those of our ancestors, that is ecstatic yet also rooted in the earth and in the history and living culture of the Celtic peoples.

So, you're like Eclectic Neopagans or something like that?

No. CR is not eclectic.

Due to a clumsy phrase in an earlier CR document ("*The CR Essay*"),[8] a comment about the value of cross-cultural comparisons was misinterpreted as advocating eclecticism. This misconception then spread in some backwaters of the Internet to such an extent as to later be repeated back to us as fact. It was surprising to hear this, to say the least, as we were accustomed to being accused of being *too* culturally focused, of having too high an academic standard and not being open enough to personal innovation for the tastes of many Neopagans.

CR was actually begun as an alternative to eclectic Neopagan traditions, and while we do allow for some innovation when there are gaps in the tradition, as much as humanly possible it is innovation based on sound, historical precedent.

See also
- ✧ Do you borrow from other cultures to "fill in the gaps"? (p. 53)
- ✧ Does CR include syncretisms? (p. 55)
- ✧ Can I be CR and still worship non-Celtic Deities? (p. 56)
- ✧ What is the difference between CR and Celtic Neopaganism? (p. 130)

I hear this is a religion, not a culture.

Perhaps you got this impression because religion does tend to be the most common topic on CR discussion lists. There is no need to work to reconstruct the non-Pagan parts of Celtic culture. As stated elsewhere, most of the Celtic cultures are still living and growing, and participation in them is an important part of CR. So we turn our efforts to where they are needed: to recovering, repairing, and reviving the polytheistic traditions that did not survive intact.

---

[8] *www.witchvox.com/trads/trad_cr.html*

See also
✧ Is this a religion, or a culture? (p. 22)
✧ How can you recreate a culture that's dead? (p. 21)

I hear you're just a political movement.

That depends on how you define "political." Most CRs would instead say that we are very concerned with **ethics**.

Some see the desire to preserve Celtic languages as a very political stance. Some of us also are or have been involved in some of the political struggles in the Celtic nations, as well as in political movements in the diaspora that are connected to these struggles.

As some Neo-Nazi and other racist groups have tried to hijack and misrepresent Celtic culture, it has become increasingly necessary to state our anti-racist position. Similarly, as most Celtic scholars have in the past focused on the more patriarchal facets of Celtic history, and severely neglected the role of women and LGBT people, many CRs feel it is necessary to rectify this bias with our research, as well as to state a pro-feminist, pro-queer position. In addition to simply honoring *all* of the ancestors, this is also in order that women and LGBT folks know they are welcome not only in the movement, but in leadership roles as well. It is akin to the practice among some Christian churches of noting that they are "a welcoming congregation." Some people who do not share these values have tried to dismiss them as "partisan politics." But to dismiss concerns about racism, sexism and homophobia as unimportant is in itself a political stance – one that shows a differing political bias, but a bias nonetheless.

See also
✧ What is the ethical basis of CR? (p. 111)
✧ Aren't all Druids men? (p. 118)
✧ You say CR is "pro-queer," but is this traditional? (p. 114)

Aren't you Pan-Celtic?

No. Individuals and groups choose a particular Celtic culture on which to base their spiritual practice.

However, most of us also *study* a variety of Celtic cultures, as well as related cultures that interacted with the Celts or have similar cosmology and practices, as this broader overview can be invaluable in helping us figure out how to reconstruct the areas that are incomplete.

See also

❖ Do you borrow from other cultures to "fill in the gaps"? (p. 53)

Isn't everyone who incorporates some degree of Celtic Research CR?

No. Various traditions, from Wicca to Neo-druidry to Eclectic Neopaganism, have always included bits of authentic Celtic material, but it was (and still is) always mixed in with material from many other cultures as well. Most Proto-CR groups started as some variety of Celtic Wiccans, or Eclectic Pagans with Celtic leanings, who then began to do serious research and to slowly incorporate larger and larger amounts of authentic material into their existing practices.

What distinguishes Proto-CR (a name which has only been applied in retrospect) from what came before was the increasing desire for authenticity, and the decision to begin the experiment of replacing non-Celtic elements – even if they were familiar and comfortable – with Celtic cosmologies and ritual structures.

By 1991 at the latest, the phrase "Celtic Reconstructionism" was coined to describe this new approach. By that point, there were a number of people using Celtic ritual structures and cosmologies, and a significant number of people had transformed their practices sufficiently to no longer resemble Wicca or genero-Paganism. With the creation of the Internet, we were now in touch with many others doing similar work, and "CR" began to be adopted by this larger group as the name for what we were doing. Celtic Reconstructionism is now recognized as both a method and an umbrella term for a diverse group of sub-traditions which, despite having some degree of uniqueness, still share this core principle of prioritizing authenticity.

The transition from other forms of Paganism to Proto-CR then to actual CR was not necessarily an easy one, nor one where every phase and step was clear-cut. It involved times of uncertainty, of facing the void left by abandoning foreign approaches and going through the neural repatterning it takes to truly live within a new cosmology, a new ritual framework, a new approach. It involved taking risks and spending time in the mists. Those who have never made this transition, who simply incorporate bits of authentic materials into a non-Celtic structure, are not CR.

How can any of you claim to have started CR?

CR began because many people felt a need for it. At various stages, there have been key people who have set an idea in motion or otherwise sparked inspiration. It could be said that without these particular thinkers, scholars, ritualists and liturgists, CR would not have happened. But it is just as true that without all the people who eventually latched on to the idea and brought their own work to the table, we wouldn't be where we are today.

Part of the traditional job of the Celtic poet or storyteller is to remember the history of the community, and the names of those whose work deserves to be remembered.

I want to call myself CR and you can't stop me.

Obviously, the individual words "Celtic" and "Reconstructionist" existed long before anyone thought to combine them as a phrase and apply them to a particular Pagan tradition. But as CR coalesced as a movement and community, many people began using the term to describe a similar approach and, as they developed, similar traditions.

So, yes, it has come to refer to a specific thing: a community of people, and the culture, beliefs and practices these people share. This means calling oneself CR if one doesn't share the core principles and traditions of CR, and if one isn't part of the CR community, is inaccurate, inappropriate, and somewhat incomprehensible. It makes no more sense than calling yourself a Hindu if you are actually a Methodist.

Actually, the founders of the tradition are surprised that some non-CRs want to call themselves CR. One of the reasons we chose the name was because it was boring and we assumed no one would want to steal it.

See also
✧ Isn't everyone who incorporates some degree of Celtic Research CR? (p. 66)

Now that I'm a Celt, shall I pick a tartan for my group to wear?

Becoming involved in the CR community doesn't automatically make you "a Celt." Nor do all people involved in the Celtic communities wear tartan. The oldest tartan patterns are specific to individual ancestral *clanns*, and are really only relevant to Gaelic varieties of CR. It is seen as quite inappropriate to simply choose a family tartan and wear it unless you were born, adopted, or married into that family.

There are some non-family tartans from Scotland, Ireland, and the diaspora, and those who are not a member of a family *clann* are in *some* cases welcome to wear one of these. These include national or district tartans and tartans designed for particular groups, occasions and occupations. It should also be noted that modern tartans can be registered by anyone with a design and enough money. There are "official" tartans for the US, Canada, Australia and other nations, as well as Japanese corporate tartans – all created and registered in the 20th and 21st centuries.

Out of respect for the living and historical cultures, if you want to wear tartan, you should familiarize yourself with the history and customs surrounding it. Like in other Celtic matters, if you show up at an event wearing tartan you will be expected to know what it means and be able to explain why you are wearing it. For instance, many people who sell tartan will say anyone can wear the military Black Watch tartan, as it is not the tartan of a particular family or region; however, you will want to familiarize yourself with the history of this (actually British) regiment and decide if you support their military policies and past actions before deciding to publicly align yourself with them. Similarly, many feel that district tartans should only be worn by those with significant knowledge of, and historical connection to, that particular district. Worn one way, tartan sashes indicate that you are a regular member of a certain *clann*; worn another way, that you married out of your original *clann* but still wish to wear the tartan of your birth- or adoptive-family; yet another way indicates that you are the chieftain of the *clann* – something very serious and likely to be contested (or laughed at) if you are not the legitimate Chief of the Name.

Tartan is not actually ancient. Though the ancient Celts probably wore clothing patterned in checks and stripes and dyed with the colors provided by their local flora and fauna, the modern, codified designs probably only date back to the sixteenth century at the earliest, and many designs are of far more recent origin (such as the many tartans that were only created in the nineteenth, twentieth and twenty-first centuries). However, tartan has been a part of some of the Celtic cultures for multiple generations now, and those of us who participate in the living cultures do sometimes wear it or include it on altars that honor particular ancestors.

See also

✧ What do you mean by "Celtic"? (p. 18)

Do you guys paint yourselves with woad?

No, not really. And our ancestors probably didn't, either. While it's possible woad was one of many pigments used for temporary body painting, it really does not work well as a body paint, and it fails miserably as a **tattoo pigment**.[9]

Tattooing does appear to be common among CRs, particularly tattoos of traditional Celtic designs. Others, especially those who cannot be tattooed for some reason, do seem to be fond of the occasional bodypaint for decorative or spiritual reasons, but again, this is a personal preference and not necessarily part of the religion.

Why would anyone want to try to bring back the Iron Age?

We don't. We're all very fond of indoor plumbing, central heating, modern medicines, eyeglasses and computers. It's the spiritual and philosophical ideals of Iron Age Celtic society that we're interested in, not recreating it down to the last parasite and drafty roundhouse. Even those who get asked this the most, the homesteader-types, are more than happy to explore modern sustainable technology rather than going back to how our ancestors farmed. There's a lot we can learn from Iron Age society, but what CR tries to do is understand what Celtic religions

---

[9] *http://www.cyberpict.net/sgathan/essays/woad.htm*

would look like now if they'd been uninterrupted since then, not to take society back to that point in history.

How can you practice a religion and still claim to believe in science?

Religion and science don't have to be in conflict. We take mythology and creation stories as metaphor rather than sources of scientific and historical fact. Mythology holds great spiritual and psychological truth where science often presents empirical, physical truths. That said, new theories are being developed in different scientific fields all the time, and science has yet to account for all phenomena in the universe.

Both psycho-spiritual truths and physical truths are necessary for an understanding of the universe we live in. Because CR doesn't have an investment in the literal truth of our mythologies, we can appreciate their spiritual truths without experiencing the dissonance of having to choose a spiritual truth over an empirical truth or vice versa.

Who can initiate me into your super-duper secret tradition handed down from the early mists of time? You are the "hidden children of the Goddess," right?

One of the most annoying theories that we face is the belief that Wicca was the secret stuff that the Celts were forbidden to write down and that anything remembered by the broader, non-occult, living culture was only there for the "ordinary people" who weren't initiates of the hidden traditions. This is sometimes referred to as the "hidden children of the Goddess" theory.

This theory flies in the face of historical fact. Gerald Gardner created Wicca in the first half of the 20th century. It's true that he drew from earlier sources, but very little of what he used were Celtic sources. Wicca owes more to Hinduism and the Masons than to Celtic religions. In fact, the basic structures and expectations of Wicca and Wicca-based genero-Paganism conflict with Celtic cosmology.

While there are strains of occult belief or techniques that have influenced CR, that influence tends to be limited, and those beliefs or techniques only used as markers for what sorts of things we're trying to find in the ancient and living traditions of the Celts.

Some of the mystics among us use techniques that are not always found in the mainstream of the living Celtic cultures, but if they are used it is with caution and without any inclusion of non-Celtic beliefs. This is discussed in more detail in the **Do you borrow from other cultures to "fill in the gaps"?** (p. 53) answer.

When Wiccans continue to insist that their non-Celtic traditions are actually Celtic, it can lead to a type of cultural imperialism – with Wiccan beliefs and practices being adopted by well-meaning people and presented as Celtic, while the actual Celtic traditions and beliefs fall into obscurity. Even residents of the Celtic nations and the diaspora are not immune to this, and this unintentional cultural imperialism has sometimes even resulted in Wiccan misinformation being presented at Celtic cultural events as "the real deal."

Any "secret" tradition that is encountered that clashes with known Celtic cosmology, culture, language, tradition, etc., should be treated with skepticism. More on this can be found in

✧ That's not how my (*insert family member here*) taught me to honor (*insert figure of choice here*)! (p. 62)

✧ Why do CRs hate Wicca and Wiccans? (p. 77).

Do you use the Celtic Tree Calendar and Celtic Astrology?

No. Neither of these actually have anything to do with any of the early Celtic peoples. The "Celtic" Tree Calendar is the creation of Robert Graves in his 1946 "work of poetic imagination," *The White Goddess*, and the creation of so-called "Celtic astrology" is even more recent (and based upon Graves' fabricated tree calendar).

While sacred trees do play a part in Celtic myth and folklore, and many CRs incorporate this older tree lore as part of their work, it is a different system than either of the above-mentioned, recent fabrications. Similarly, there are old manuscripts that point to possibilities of an ancient Celtic view of astronomy and astrology, but these are nothing like what has been popularized as "tree astrology," and the information is still rather obscure as little of it has been published in English.

For a good discussion of the alleged tree calendar and a debunking of the tree astrology that grew out of it, see Peter

Berresford Ellis's article, *"The Fabrication of 'Celtic Astrology'."*[10] Another article by Ellis, *"Early Irish Astrology: An Historical Argument,"*[11] discusses what is known about the possible existence of a pre-Christian Irish astrological system, which used native names and concepts (none of them trees) for the planets and constellations.

Aren't there oghams in America too?

No. While Barry Fell and some of his followers in the Epigraphic Society and other groups have made such claims, particularly in Fell's 1976 book *America B.C.*, there is no physical evidence that any Celtic people arrived in North America before the arrival of Columbus. It can be conclusively proved that the Norse people arrived in pre-Columbian Canada, for they left physical evidence of their inhabitation in Newfoundland – artifacts, structures, and written accounts preserved in other countries about their colonies. By contrast, there is no physical evidence that the Irish or Scots ever came to North America in pre-Columbian times, and the *immrama* voyage accounts of early Irish literature are far more easily read as Otherworldly adventures than an account of actual landings in North America. If the Irish or the Scots had arrived prior to Columbus, we would expect to find potsherds, buttons, weapons, drop-spindles, and a wide variety of other physical items left behind in trash heaps, broken in fields of battle, or in the remains of dwellings. None of these things exist.

While there are some stone structures, especially in the Northeastern US, that are built in a "beehive" style common to Celtic cultures, there is absolutely no evidence that they are pre-Columbian. As the First Nations people of these regions state the structures resemble nothing from their cultures, it can reasonably be assumed that these stone structures were probably built by Irish or Scottish immigrants, who came in the usual waves of later immigration from those countries. None of these structures have anything resembling *ogham* carved on them.

Fell's "research" methods are deeply flawed and his conclusions are nothing more than fiction. For an in-depth

---

[10] http://cura.free.fr/xv/13ellis2.html
[11] http://www.radical-astrology.com/irish/miscellany/ellis.html

discussion and debunking of his claims, including an analysis of how he comes to his "translations" of his alleged *ogham* texts, "**A Linguistic Analysis of Some West Virginia Petroglyphs**"[12] by Monroe Oppenheimer and Willard Wirtz is extremely useful, along with the links at the bottom of that page. It should be noted that Fell was not a Celtic scholar and knew next to nothing about Celtic languages, archaeology, or history. He was a professor of Marine Biology – a discipline quite useless in tracing language and inscriptions, or in dealing with archaeological sites. The fact that someone has a degree in one field is no guarantee that they know what they're talking about in another.

The most distressing aspect of Fell's assertions is the underlying, essentially racist assumption that the First Nations tribes were incapable of making petroglyphs of their own, observing the universal fact of solstitial and equinoctial solar phenomena, or of building any stone structures that might vaguely resemble European standing stones or other megalithic structures. It's akin to asserting that the ancient Egyptians were incapable of building the pyramids themselves and concluding that, therefore, aliens did it. Human beings are extremely inventive and capable, regardless of their origins. Let us give credit where it's due and leave the science fiction and fantasy for novels.

See also
✧ What is this Ogham stuff you keep mentioning? (p. 57)

What about the Four Treasures and Four Cities, don't they go in the cardinal directions?

No, the Invasions of Ireland texts are clear that the four cities of the Túatha Dé Danann are located "in the North of the world" or perhaps the sky. There was no correlation of the Four Treasures with the four cardinal directions or Classical four "elements" until the 19th century, when William Butler Yeats and others were trying to fit Irish mythology into a Golden Dawn-style system called The Castle of Heroes.

It should also be noted that the Four Treasures are really only relevant to Irish Reconstructionist Paganism, as they are not found at all in Welsh, Gaulish, or other Celtic mythologies.

---

[12] *http://cwva.org/ogam_rebutal/wirtz.html*

Aren't you CRs in North America stealing cultural elements from Native Americans/the First Nations?

This question is somewhat baffling, as one of the main reasons we started CR was to **avoid** the type of cultural theft that we saw (and still see) going on in the "Celtic Shamanism" and Eclectic Neopagan groups.

Our Celtic ancestors had their own cultural and religious beliefs and practices, and we still have the living Celtic cultures which, while not thoroughly polytheistic, are still vital in terms of culture and community. We are interested in rebuilding what our own people lost, not in stealing from others.

The problem of cultural theft is a serious one, though, and is rampant in the Neopagan communities. It is largely due to issues of cultural theft that most of us no longer identify as part of the Neopagan community. CR as a whole is committed to respecting the cultures of First Nations peoples, as well as respecting the desires of the traditional peoples of those communities to set their own definitions, boundaries and standards. Many of us actively support the *Lakota Declaration of War*, as well as doing what we can to help out *First Nations groups* who work to expose *"Plastic Shamans"*[13] and other frauds and exploiters of Native American spirituality. We also work in our own communities to educate people about issues of cultural sovereignty, and cultural integrity vs. cultural theft.

In researching ancient Celtic cultures and religions, it is true that we have found some practices that are similar to *some* of the practices of *some* First Nations cultures. However, this does not mean those practices are identical, universal, or in any way interchangeable. Most cultures, worldwide, have some methods of seeking inspiration, of reaching for communion with the divine. Many cultures have a history of heraldry or other ways of identifying, and connecting, with the symbolism of the natural world. Ecstatic practices do not always equal "shamanism," and no one culture is the sole arbiter of ecstatic states. However, individual cultures, especially the traditionals and elders of those cultures, **do** own their traditions, and have a right to protect them from those who are not part of their culture or community. There

---

[13] Please see the online version of this FAQ at *http://www.paganachd.com/faq* for current linkage on these three items.

is a danger in acknowledging the similarities that are there, as some who desire to create a sort of eclectic, "Celtic Shamanism" have often seized on these small similarities and used them as an excuse for the types of abuses we in CR are trying so hard to avoid. This is why we do our best to make a distinction between our approach and that of eclectics and "*shame-ons*."[14]

See also

✧ Do you practice Celtic shamanism? (p. 133)
✧ Who do I pay to be initiated into Celtic Shamanism? (p. 134)
✧ Do you borrow from other cultures to "fill in the gaps"? (p. 53)
✧ Does CR include syncretisms? (p. 55)
✧ Can I be CR and still worship non-Celtic Deities? (p. 56)
✧ Why are you racist? (p. 61)

So isn't CR just cultural theft from the Celtic cultures?

CR's relationship with the living and historical Celtic cultures differs from cultural theft in crucial ways.

Cultural theft involves removing pieces from a culture and using them out of context in a foreign cultural matrix. Very often, the foreign culture will have tried to wipe out the culture being robbed, and this theft of religious traditions is a continuation of that destruction and imperialism. In contrast, CR specifically requires that the Celtic cultural matrix be the framework in which we function as a tradition and community.

While we can't speak to every thing that has been done by every individual who has ever claimed to be CR, we hope we have made it clear in this document that preservation of and respect for the living Celtic cultures is a core part of CR. Anyone who is simply stealing bits of Celtic culture and inserting them into a non-Celtic format is not CR, no matter what they may claim, no matter how they may dress it up in velvet cloaks or appliquéd bits of knotwork and tartan. CR strongly focuses on participating in and giving back to the Celtic cultures, not just taking from them. Many CRs support Celtic arts and artists, language study groups, political causes, and charity work. We insist upon a respectful and

---

[14] Please see the online version of this FAQ at *http://www.paganachd.com/faq* for current linkage.

giving relationship with the Celtic cultures, not a pillaging of them.

Being a part of any ethnic diaspora can be a difficult thing. Many of us have felt rootless at one point or another, and it is this feeling that makes many Americans in particular prone to cultural theft. If someone was raised with no particular sense of cultural identity, it can be hard for them to understand issues of cultural sovereignty and cultural integrity. One of the missions of CR is to help people understand these issues so they do not behave offensively.

CR was begun as an alternative to the cultural theft that is rampant in the Neopagan communities. Before CR, and still in the Neopagan and Newage communities, all kinds of non-Celtic practices and beliefs were being misrepresented as Celtic. But we were looking for something authentically Celtic, that honored our ancestors without dishonoring anyone else's, and that respected and honored the living traditions.

For those of us who founded CR, becoming rooted in the ways of our ancestors was one of the main reasons we began this journey. For some it was **the** main reason. Though the CR community is welcoming to people of all ethnic and racial backgrounds and now includes members from all over the world, including people in the modern Celtic nations, it was begun by American members of the Celtic diaspora, a number of whom grew up in largely Irish- and Scottish-American communities. Among the CRs who did not grow up in the Celtic nations, some have lived in Celtic nations as adults, attended school there, and/or have good relations with friends or family members in those countries. When the ancestors of the diasporan Celts stepped off the boats or planes, they did not immediately jettison their culture, their values, or their ways of life. Some of them lived in Irish ghettos (in cities like New York, Boston and Chicago) and rural Gaelic communities (such as the Gaelic enclaves in Nova Scotia and Peoria) where some of their native traditions and languages were maintained. With the passage of time, some of our ancestors and families held on to their heritage, while others were eager to assimilate into the proverbial melting pot.

Those of us who participate in language preservation, the preservation and development of Celtic art forms, and the political struggles in the Celtic nations are doing our best to be honorable, to do our small part to give back at least as much as we take. If they are not already, we actively encourage all people interested in CR to also become involved in their local Celtic communities in a respectful and sustained way, not as tourists. We encourage them to study the language(s), to learn as much as they can about the cultures involved, to educate themselves on the history and political struggles in the Celtic nations and to support these causes as much as they are able.

The CR community is now made up of a diverse lot of people, some of whom are descended from recent Celtic immigrants, others whose ancestors have been in the diaspora for a long time, some who live in the Celtic nations, and still others who are not of Celtic heritage but are drawn to Celtic culture and wish to make a sincere contribution to the community. What we share is that we are all fully committed to establishing and continuing deep, strong relationships with the Celtic cultures as an essential dimension of our CR practice. We express hospitality and welcome diversity in our communities in the spirit of all working together to revitalize the polytheistic aspects of the Celtic cultures. All ethnic and racial backgrounds are welcome to join us, but that does not change our rootedness in Celtic culture and religion.

See also

✧ How can you recreate a culture that's dead? (p. 21)
✧ Is this a religion, or a culture? (p. 22)
✧ But, what do you mean by "The living Celtic cultures"? (p. 23)
✧ How can you claim to be a Celtic tradition if you're not immersed in the Culture? (p. 28)
✧ What is the difference between CR and Celtic Neopaganism? (p. 130)
✧ Who can initiate me into your super-duper secret tradition handed down from the early mists of time? You are the "hidden children of the Goddess," right? (p. 70)
✧ Why are you racist? (p. 61)
✧ Are you Gaelic Traditionalists? What is the difference between Traditionalism and Reconstructionism? (p. 134).

Why do CRs hate Wicca and Wiccans?

We don't, but Wicca includes a number of fundamentals which are different from those of the native Celtic religions. These include differing conceptions of divinity, cosmological organization, and many other assumptions about the spirit world and methods of interacting with it. Some Wiccans have been taught that their religion is identical to ancient Celtic religion, and have made a number of claims which are simply not supportable in a Celtic context; when corrected on these misconceptions, some have assumed that meant that CR was perforce *opposed* to Wicca in some way. In reality, it is a complex situation.

As CR is about cultural focus and cultural cohesiveness, and Wicca was compiled from an eclectic combination of beliefs, and practices from a wide variety of cultures, it has also been common for some Wiccans to not understand why we are culturally focused, and to take our decision to not be eclectic as a judgment on the inherent human worth of individuals who do choose to be eclectic. Sometimes hard feelings have resulted when, for instance, one side feels the other is doing something that is offensive in their tradition. While we try to have good relations with those with whom we may disagree, sometimes deeply-held beliefs can make it hard to be accepting of individuals whose practices we feel are culturally inappropriate.

It should be noted that books about "Celtic Wicca" are very poor sources for Celtic information and lore. These books generally describe a Wiccan framework with Celtic Deity names and concepts inserted with little regard for the original Celtic culture and context. This leads to inevitable misunderstandings. CRs have often been frustrated by the misconceptions propagated by these books.

See also

✧ Who can initiate me into your super-duper secret tradition handed down from the early mists of time? You are the "hidden children of the Goddess," right? (p. 70)

Do CRs believe all Celtic traditions should be "modernized"?

No, not all CRs believe this. CR is a diverse community. We do not all agree all the time.

For instance, there are diametrically opposed views in the community about whether it is acceptable to modernize the longstanding tradition of women flametenders for the Goddess

Bríde (aka Brigidine Orders) to now include men. Of the CRs who have participated in writing the answers to this FAQ, a majority are adamant that this traditional form of worship must remain for women only, while others believe that the modern innovation of including all genders is acceptable. Other issues in the debate include the place of men in Bríde's worship, and what dedicants to Bríde can do in a structured situation aside from flametending.

A milder example of a modernization debate is the discussion about how much Celtic land-based traditions such as tree *ogham* or *dindshenchas* should be adapted to wildly differing climates in the Celtic diaspora. While Celtic tradition contains many examples of the importance of adapting to one's local ecology and nature spirits, there is also the question of how far these adaptations can go before the tradition simply isn't Celtic anymore. When a CR is living in Australia, Arizona, or some other place with a radically different ecology from the lands where Celtic culture originally developed, some CRs believe it is more appropriate to adapt traditions for the place that you find yourself, such as choosing native trees of your bioregion for tree *ogham* or moving the dates of festivals to coincide with local natural events such as "first frost," if indeed there even is one. Others believe that it is more accurate to maintain the original associations and their historical attributes, even if they don't fit the natural cycles or climate of the place that the CR lives.

Another issue that comes up is Romano-Celtic syncretism, and how much Roman influence is acceptable in Romano-Celtic branches of CR before it becomes Roman rather than Celtic. As with other issues of syncretism and eclecticism, it can be a problem of cultures of oppression versus native cultures, and of how history is read through various lenses.

Such debates are a natural part of hammering out what it means to have a modern incarnation of a living tradition, and are not unexpected. Though in most things we endeavour for consensus, in some matters it is necessary to mention that there are differing camps on an issue, and that neither camp is perceived as speaking for the whole of the CR community.

See also
✧ What is this Ogham stuff you keep mentioning? (p. 57)
✧ Does CR include syncretisms? (p. 55)

So all CRs worship the same way?

No. It isn't actually possible for all CRs to have identical rituals and holy days. Not only are all CRs different people, but our interests and our Deities pull us toward different Celtic cultures. The fact is, different cultures within the Celtic matrix, and different cultures within the even larger and more diverse Indo-European matrices, do things in different ways, and different Deities demand different things. Languages also play a role in this, marking different cultures and different paths of approach to ritual and cosmology.

This means that, while certain basics of the frameworks may sometimes be similar, there will also be significant differences in the ways that, for instance, a Scottish-focused CR would do things compared to the way a Breton CR would do the same type of ritual. And both of these will usually be quite different from a Vedic or Hindu ritual, despite all being Indo-European cultures. In fact, due to differences in the cultures and languages, they may not do rituals for the same things or the same holy days. They certainly won't be doing them for the same Deities.

As a result, it's not wise or even useful to take a basic ritual format and just "plug in" a set of Deities based on the culture and language you want to work with today. You have to be respectful of the cultures you're working with, and of the Deities themselves. Anyone telling you that you can do "plug and play" ritual within a CR context doesn't understand what reconstruction actually means.

See also
- ✧ Isn't everyone who incorporates some degree of Celtic Research CR? (p. 66)
- ✧ Aren't you Pan-Celtic? (p. 65)
- ✧ I want to call myself CR and you can't stop me. (p. 67)

I've heard that you are mean to people who have questions. Why is that?

Some CRs or CR communities may have acquired this reputation because we don't suffer fools, liars or the overly credulous easily. Everyone was a beginner in CR at one time. Lack of knowledge is understandable and expected. However, if someone pretends to have knowledge or experience they obviously do not have, they are rarely tolerated for long.

CR very much has the motto of "Show me." If someone comes up with a new and novel explanation for historic or pre-historic Celtic practices, they should be prepared to provide some proof, either in the archaeological record or through research. CRs do not accept "I say it's so, so it is so." CRs generally expect you to cite academic sources and present a reasoned argument for radically different interpretations of any ancient Celtic practice, society, or belief.

While personal inspiration is also an important part of CR, when something is not supported by the lore, it is necessary to indicate this as UPG.

Many people new to CR are surprised to hear this question, as they swear they've never received uncompassionate or harsh treatment from any CRs. It does seem that the attitude with which the new person approaches the community largely determines the reception they will receive.

Polite questions are always welcome. It's just when people are impolite or overly demanding that the folks used to fielding the questions can get cranky. But if we didn't like answering questions, we'd hardly be writing a FAQ, now would we?

See also

✧ What is this UPG thing I keep hearing about? (p. 48)

Chapter Five

Theology

Do you worship The Goddess?

As polytheists, we worship a number of Goddesses. And even some Gods!

Actually, this question is based on the common Neopagan (and especially Wiccan) concept that all Gods & Goddesses are fractional parts of a greater Goddess and God, (or a single, monotheistic Goddess), and that these many, individual Deities are merely aspects of a greater "archetype" that can be swapped around willy-nilly. This goes completely against the CR perspective that the Deities are real and separate individuals. It also goes against our belief that different cultures have their own unique Deities and religious beliefs about Them. In fact, there are known conflicts among some of the various Celtic Deities, which would make no sense if they were all part of some über-Godhead.

So, in answer to the question, we do not worship "The Goddess," as that is simply not the way we perceive the cosmos. It is not a Celtic theology (or "thealogy") and we do not accept that any such all-powerful, monotheistic being, if one exists, has any meaningful existence in our sphere of worship.

See also

✧ What is the difference between CR and Celtic Neopaganism? (p. 130)
✧ Why do CRs hate Wicca and Wiccans? (p. 77)

Which Gods do you worship?

That depends a lot on the individual and the Celtic culture that draws them most strongly. There were hundreds of Celtic Deities from dozens of tribal cultures throughout the early Celtic period. Irish and Scottish Reconstructionists might worship Brighid or the Dagda, the Morrígan or Manannán mac Lir. Welsh Reconstructionists might worship Llew Llaw Gyffes or Cerridwen, or Rhiannon or Gwynn ap Nudd. Gaulish Reconstructionists would be more interested in Taranis, Epona, Belenus or Rosmerta. As a polytheistic tradition, most CRs will honor a number of Deities, though they may be closest to a particular one.

So you worship all the Celtic Deities?

Not exactly. Rather than being Pan-Celtic, CRs focus on a particular Celtic culture (Gaelic, Gaulish, Welsh, etc). Even within a specific cultural grouping, not all Deities are seen to get along with one another, at least not all the time. Also, given the hundreds of known Celtic Deities and the likelihood of there being more local Deities as yet unknown, honoring each one individually would be extremely time-consuming and entirely impractical. Most CRs will have a subset of Deities with whom they have strong alliances, while still offering respect to the broader spectrum of spiritual beings they may encounter.

So should I just pick a Matron or Patron from a list of Deities and swear oaths to Them?

Among CRs who are sworn to a particular matron or patron Deity, you usually find the belief that we don't choose these Deities, They choose us. Free will is still a factor, but there are clear examples in the lore of the misfortunes that can come to those who refuse this call.

Not all CRs are oathbound to a particular Deity or even believe that such an arrangement is a desirable thing. For others it is a core part of their spirituality and identity, a source of guidance and strength. Whichever view one holds, embarking on that sort of relationship without ample time to get to know that Deity, and understand what They ask of you, would be incredibly foolish.

You wouldn't just choose a random stranger out of the phone book and marry them, now would you?

The Celts worshipped a huge number of Deities. Some were very local, perhaps only concerned with the members of a particular tribe or the inhabitants of a small bioregion. Other Deities became very popular and were worshipped by many tribes in many parts of the Celtic lands. No modern Celt even knows the names of all the Deities Who were honored by their ancestors, let alone worships Them all. So even among those who don't have a particular matron or patron Deity, they will have a smaller number of Deities with Whom they are on more familiar terms than others.

I want to do a ritual, which Deity should I use?

CRs don't presume to "use" Deities.

The idea, common among many Neopagans and occultists, that Deities are just created thoughtforms, interchangeable archetypes, energy batteries or psychic pets, is generally derived from Ceremonial Magic or modern psychology, particularly the Jungian-influenced branches. It is not a part of Celtic religion.

Rather than attempting to "use" or order around divine beings, we seek to know Them and build relationships of mutual respect and affection. Much like making a human friend, these things take time and the relationship must be maintained and treated with care. While the Celtic Deities like to see us take pride in ourselves and our accomplishments, and do not expect us to grovel, neither do They want to be taken for granted or treated disrespectfully.

Historically, some interactions with the Deities seem to have been of a "contractual" nature, involving some form of reciprocal transaction. For example, most of the surviving Celtic altars have inscriptions indicating they were placed there in fulfillment of a vow – as a form of "payment" to the Deity for services rendered. This is not to say that all interactions with the Deities and spirits were, or are, on the basis of *quid pro quo* but, historically speaking, it does appear that many of them were.

What about this ancestor reverence and land spirit stuff?

There is a lot of good evidence that both ancestors and the various spirits of the land and waters were revered by the early Celtic tribes. Local rivers and springs were seen as the embodiment of the divine. Mountains and mounds were believed to be the abode of Deities and spirits. Offerings were left for land and house spirits well into modern times, and still are today in many Celtic areas as a part of the living folk tradition from which CR draws its best inspiration.

We believe that land spirits, ancestors and Deities are all part of a community and continuity of spirit, rather than being separate orders of being. Venerated ancestors may become guardian spirits of a particular place, or rise to a level of Deity at some point, while many Deities show signs of originally having been local spirits of rivers or other natural places. As mortal human beings, we are a part of that continuity as well, and our relationship with the ancestors, the spirits and the Deities is one of family and tribal affiliation, as well as mutual affection and respect.

When we refer to the ancestors, we are not just speaking of our blood relations. We value the broader communities in which we live, and the many people who have had an important influence on our lives. Therefore, most CRs tend to refer to all of our beloved dead as our ancestors, not just those who are related to us physically. One piece of CR liturgy in use addresses the ancestors as,

> You who have walked this land before us
> You who have walked this path before us,
> You whose bodies, minds and spirits
> gave form to our bodies, minds and spirits.
> All of you whose lives have made our lives possible.
> > (K.P. NicDhàna of *Pàganachd Bhandia*
> > and *Nigheanan nan Cailleachan*)

In this spirit, most of us will find that, although we are approaching the ancestors in a CR style, not all the ancestors on our altars are Celts. Generally, ancestors are glad to be remembered, and not always picky about the exact format we use. However, other ancestors can become demanding, and be specific in what they want. In these cases, some CRs of diverse ancestry may find that their ancestor altar is the place where some degree of non-Celtic symbology and approach does come into play, if it is what their ancestors request of them. Others have found their ancestors to be so excited by the attention, that they have played a large part in pushing us to develop CR. Whatever our individual results, whatever our individual ancestry, CR is inclusive of all of our diverse ancestors, be they of the body, mind or spirit.

See also

✧ What do you think happens when you die? (p. 89)

So where do the fairies and sídhe fit into this?

There are various Otherworldly beings who, over the centuries, have been referred to as the Fairies, the *Áes Sídhe*, *Aos Sí*, or *Daoine-Sìth*, among other names. Opinions differ, but the living Fairy Faith from which we draw much inspiration has variously applied these names to the ancestors, the spirits of nature, or even later, literary versions of the Goddesses and Gods Themselves.

While CRs seldom use the English term "Fairies" to describe them, we do realize that this is a common term used to represent those who many of us know as the *Aos Sí* or *Daoine-Sìth* - "the people of peace," or "the people of the mounds." The fact that they are described in the lore as living "underhill" in the mounds is seen by some to indicate that they are indeed the ancestors, living in the burial mounds, and by others to indicate they could be some sort of chthonic Deities. We may also choose to refer to them as "The Good Neighbors," "The Good Folk" or simply "The Folk" as is traditional in Gaelic areas, as it is believed that speaking of them might draw their attention and, if so, it's best to imply that they might be kind. This practice may vary greatly, however, as some feel more comfortable speaking of them than do others.

The trepidation some feel about referring to them too openly, as evident in lore and SPG, is that not all the *Aos Sí* are particularly friendly towards us. Some might not want dealings with humans at all, others may be particular as to whom they want to deal with. Some spirits of nature may be hostile towards all humans for the actions of some, especially in cases where the earth has been harmed. In these cases they may be regarded as Outsiders. In order to co-exist peacefully with angry spirits, we might make treaty offerings, as noted in **You talk a lot about the role of the Outsiders. What do you mean by that?** (p. 91). For those who are friendly we may make offerings to them a bit closer to home and, by offering this hospitality, help strengthen that friendship.

While in the Celtic countries it may be appropriate to refer to all the land, nature and house spirits, as some type of *Aos Sí* or *Daoine-Sìth*, many in the diaspora feel that using these terms for all spirits in the lands where we now live would be presumptuous and inaccurate. Some of these spirits might be *Aos Sí* or *Daoine-Sìth* who came over with the human population, but others are more likely Native spirits or perhaps something else entirely.

Among those who believe the *Aos Sí* are a particular class of semi-divine being, many believe that there are strong connections between the *Aos Sí* and the Deities, with some Goddesses and Gods having *Aos Sí* bloodlines or actually being *Aos Sí* Themselves. To an extent this may seem to relate to the Christian belief that the Deities of the Túatha Dé Danann became "diminished" into the *Aos Sí*, however, it also dismisses the idea by noting that only some of the Túatha Dé Danann always were *Aos Sí* and that others are not and never were.

There are also those who believe that some of our ancestors might have "gone underhill" to join The Folk when they died, and that this is a separate place than where most of the ancestors go.

Note: In many English-language sources, the fairy folk are referred to simply as "the *Sídhe*," but this is incorrect. This oft-reproduced mistake probably resulted from English-speakers' attempts to abbreviate the Old Irish phrase *Áes Sídhe*, or similar nomenclature for "the people of the mounds," without understanding Irish grammar. In actual Gaelic usage, only the mounds are called *síd[h]e*, *síthe* or *sìtheananan*, while the spirits who inhabit the mounds are referred to as "the people of the mounds": **Aos Sí** or **Daoine-Sìth**. For more on this see the glossary.

See also

- ✧ What do you think happens when you die? (p. 89)
- ✧ What about this ancestor reverence and land spirit stuff? (p. 86)

✧ Offerings seem to be a really important part of all these rituals. How do I make offerings? (p. 107)
✧ What is this UPG thing I keep hearing about? (p. 48)

What do you think happens when you die?

That depends on the individual CR practitioner. Many of us believe in reincarnation, and there is evidence in the source texts from within and outside of Celtic cultures suggesting that the early Celts of many tribes believed in reincarnation and/or transmigration of souls. It is said that the belief in reincarnation was strong enough that contracts could be made to be fulfilled in future lives. There is, however, no indication of a belief that *not* reincarnating was either possible or desirable, as is found in Hindu and Buddhist beliefs, where the spiritual goal is to get off the wheel of death and rebirth.

Some believe that we go to the land of the dead when we die, variously identified as the House of Donn (*Teach Duinn*) or the Land of Youth (*Tír na nÓg*) over the sea to the west of Ireland. These Otherworld lands would go by different names in different Celtic languages and cultures. There is evidence that it was believed the ancestors dwelt beneath the ground in the *Síde* (burial or "fairy" mounds) or perhaps under the sea with Manannán mac Lír. Given time, people might leave these Otherworld lands and return to the lands of the living, often as a descendant in a family line, or that of a beloved friend, but possibly also in a non-human form; for instance, as an animal or other creature.

Some CRs have developed death rites and have performed rituals to help departed souls move on. Our beloved dead are honored, remembered with a place on the ancestor altar and given regular offerings to help them progress. After they have been among the dead for a while, they are sometimes asked for help and guidance. It is possible some of the Deities were once human ancestors, and that an honored ancestor can rise to a place of considerable power in the spirit world.

See also
✧ Offerings seem to be a really important part of all these rituals. How do I make offerings? (p. 107)

What do you mean when you say that it's not a dualistic religion?

Dualistic religions, such as Zoroastrianism and Christianity, hold the belief that there are opposing forces in the world, one good and one evil, who battle over Creation for dominance. We can find no evidence that pre-Christian Celtic belief perceived the spiritual realm in this fashion. Most Celtic Deities are depicted as being capable of both virtuous acts and destructive ones. Some of the figures in mythology are more prone to play the tester than others, such as Bricriu, but even he is not portrayed as evil.

Another sense of the word "dualistic" that is sometimes used could be better described as "gender polarity," or the assumption that a God and Goddess must be invoked at each ritual of a certain level of importance in order for there to be a proper "balance." This is not a Celtic belief. We are unaware of any evidence that, for example, An Daghda and An Mhor-Ríoghain were invoked by the druids to bless the bonfires every *Oíche Shamhna*, although some Neopagans have made that sort of assumption based on a tale where these two Deities had sex before one battle which took place at that time of year. We also do not see echoes of this fixation on "gender polarity" in what is known of other Indo-European religious rituals. It is a common pattern in many Wiccan traditions that is sometimes carried over into some people's practices when they turn to Celtic traditions. It is, however, clearly borrowed from Wicca.

One duality that does exist in Celtic patterns is the concept of the light and dark halves of the year, often referred to as *samos/giamos*; that concept was generalized by some Celtic peoples into a larger philosophical model of revealed/active and hidden/incubatory things. There are indications that, in some strains of Celtic belief, there were gender assignments made to each half, but due to the different perspectives on gender modern Celts and CRs possess compared to their ancestors, these assignments are not as meaningful as they once were. As a counterexample to the idea that each half was always associated with one of the two genders, in Scotland the light and dark halves were assigned not to gender, but to age, with the Cailleach as Winter Hag ruling the dark half of the year and Bríde as Spring Maiden or Summer Queen ruling the light. There are other possible examples of same-gender dualities of this sort, as well. Furthermore, it is the opinion of at least a few CR theologians that rigid gender assignment to the two halves is not necessary to understanding them, and in fact may impede a clear understanding of many common symbolic motifs.

See also
  ✧ Is it Samhain, Samhuinn or Samain? Why all these different spellings? (p. 58)
  ✧ What holidays do you celebrate? Don't you do the eightfold wheel of the year? (p. 94)

You talk a lot about the role of the Outsiders. What do you mean by that?

When CRs refer to "Outsiders" it may refer to one, or both, of two things.

It could mean Outsider spirits and Deities, which has become for many a way to describe those Beings we do not worship or offer to in our own spaces. This may include any Gods or spirits who we simply do not worship, as they are from other cultures. It may also include *Aos Sí*, Fomorian or Fir Bolg beings who may be hostile to humans, as opposed to other *Aos Sí*, Fomorians or Fir Bolg who might be more friendly to humans or to particular humans. In some cases, the beings may be nature spirits who have an (often well-deserved) dislike of humans due to their past experiences with disrespectful people, or psychotic ghosts who are not capable of being healed. Some CRs strive to make "treaty" with such beings, usually at the boundaries of their property or some distance from a ritual site. This is done to make an agreement that if the spirits take the offering, They are promising to not disrupt the home or ritual.

A significant number of CRs also refer to ourselves as "Outsiders." "Outlaw" might be an appropriate name as well, but may be misunderstood in contemporary society. A number of us feel we would not fit as civilized adults into any of the categories of Iron Age Celtic culture and instead find inspiration in the *fianna* lore and other stories of those who lived outside of mainstream society. We may identify more as "mad mystics" and "warrior-poets" living among other unusual people in the wilderness, even if for many it is an urban wilderness.

The liminal, the misty, the changeable, all are key factors in Celtic thought. Those who walk on the edges, or who participate in roles or activities others may see as polar opposites, are a traditional part of our history as well as important to modern Celts.

Some believe that at this stage in our history, most CRs could be considered "Outsiders" to one extent or another, as there is not yet a thoroughly CR society to fit into. This is in a way fitting, if one considers the idea that among the ancient Celts many adolescent boys (and possibly girls) may have spent time in outlaw warbands before attaining their adult status. CR as a movement and community is still in its youth and could be argued to be "not yet fit for society," as it were. However, even as more structure develops over the coming years, there are some of us who will likely always see ourselves as Outsiders and prefer a highly individualistic existence to anything we perceive as overly codified and rigid.

Being "Outside" is also a matter of degree and often not clearly defined. The *fianna*, for instance, were Outsiders who protected the society from far more dangerous Outsiders.

See also

✧ Offerings seem to be a really important part of all these rituals. How do I make offerings? (p. 107)

Chapter Six

Ritual

How do you create sacred space?

Most CRs feel sacred space is not made, it is found. As a religion connected to the earth and the spirits of nature, we are likely to seek out a wild place that feels powerful to us, then communicate with the spirits of that place to establish a working relationship based on hospitality and mutual respect. In these cases, through our repeated offerings and reverence, and sometimes through the building of shrines, the place becomes even more sacred.

Like other sorts of Pagans, we also try to make more neutral spaces sacred, or find the sacred in unlikely places and build upon it. Most CRs have household shrines, dedicated to various Deities, ancestors and other spirits. When beginning a ritual – whether it be a simple offering with prayers or a more elaborate group rite – many CRs will first purify and bless themselves and the space. This is often called *saining* ("blessing, sanctifying"), and can be done with the smoke of sacred herbs like juniper, with water or flame, with song and poetry, or simply with the energy of the ritualists. Many use a combination of all of these methods.

Protection of the space, when needed, is generally accomplished through the aid of Deities and spirits, and the use of traditional items such as sacred trees, flame and herbs. This seems especially true of those working in an Insular format. If a boundary of some sort is desired, most CRs are likely to choose naturally-occurring boundaries such as a stream or grove of trees, or to meditate on the concept of the edge and the center, and the

Ninth Wave of the ocean which is the boundary between this world and the Otherworld. Some CRs, especially those following a Gaulish model, like to create a physical boundary of some sort around their ritual spaces (such as a ditch or wall), or perhaps a temporary boundary of energy. Perhaps the majority of CRs create no boundary at all, and see the energy of the ritual as sufficiently contained and present, or needing no containment at all, as the purpose is not to wall out spirits but to create relationships with them. In cases where the spirits are not helpful or peaceful, and an alliance cannot be made, ritual actions and offerings are often made to create a treaty of non-interference with them.

See also

⬦ Offerings seem to be a really important part of all these rituals. How do I make offerings? (p. 107)

⬦ You talk a lot about the role of the Outsiders. What do you mean by that? (p. 91)

What holidays do you celebrate? Don't you do the eightfold wheel of the year?

Folks following insular Celtic paths generally celebrate Samhain (*Oíche Shamhna*), Imbolc (*Lá Fhéile Bríde*), Bealtaine (*Lá Bealtaine*) and Lúnasa (*Lá Lúnasa*), though they may call these festivals by other names, depending on the Celtic culture in which they are working. Other individual holy days may be added, depending on the Deities or spirits important to the celebrants. For instance, followers of Manannán mac Lír might celebrate His holy day near the summer solstice, which was traditionally the time when the Manx paid their rent to Him for the island. Scottish CRs may celebrate *Latha na Cailliche*, March 25/Spring Equinox, the date when Brìghde finally triumphs over the Cailleach and begins Her reign over the warm half of the year.

CR as a whole does not follow an eightfold wheel of the year. Gaulish CRs follow the Coligny calendar as best they can, but again, that calendar doesn't offer an eightfold cycle of holy days.

At *Oíche Shamhna*, our new year, we pay our respects to our ancestors. *Lá Fhéile Bríde* marks the first stirrings of spring, and is one of Bríde's festivals. *Lá Bealtaine* is a fertility festival when the hawthorn blooms and fields are ploughed and planted. *Lá Lúnasa* is a first harvest festival marked by athletic games in honor of

Lugh's foster mother Tailltiu, and rainstorms are seen as the presence of Lugh at the rites.

CRs may celebrate the holidays on the calendar date or follow a lunar calendar which centers the festival around the full moon of that season. Perhaps most CRs choose the date for celebration based on changes in local weather and landscape (first frost, spring thaw, blooming of the hawthorn trees, ripening of the blueberries or blackberries, or other phenomena). And a modern, but important, tradition followed by many is to celebrate the festival on The Date When Everyone Can Make It (usually the weekend closest to one of the above phenomena).

See also

✧ Is it Samhain, Samhuinn or Samain? Why all these different spellings? (p. 58)
✧ What do you do for Samhain? (p. 97)
✧ What do you do for Imbolc? (p. 98)
✧ What do you do for Bealtaine? (p. 100)
✧ What do you do for Lúnasa? (p. 103)

What kinds of rituals do you have?

Like any other spiritual path, we have rituals for life's passages. We celebrate handfastings, child blessings, burial rituals and adulthood rites. Additionally, we have seasonal rites that usually involve feasting and offerings, and are held at the turning points of the year. For the folks on Gaelic paths these would be Samhain (*Oíche Shamhna*), Imbolc (*Lá Fhéile Bríde*), Bealtaine (*Lá Bealtaine*) and Lúnasa (*Lá Lúnasa*), or the Brythonic equivalents for other Insular Celtic paths.

A common CR practice is to familiarize yourself with the land you live on, its wildlife and natural seasonal cycles, and synchronize your seasonal festivals around the changes that happen on the land where you live. CRs in the Southern Hemisphere will be observing different changes than CRs in the Northern Hemisphere, and this should be taken into account when planning seasonal rites. We have culturally based community rituals that are primarily celebratory in nature, and smaller, more mystical or ecstatic rites.

We also make rituals of everyday things, from purifications upon rising or before going to bed to daily renewal of food and drink offerings on our household or personal altars. Candles might be lit on shrines for the dead, or to ask for healing for friends or relatives who are ill. We also have more involved rituals for healing and for protection that we use when necessary.

Some individuals or groups may have specialized rituals, for instance periodic devotionals to different Deities. Based upon the historical orders of women flamekeepers, there are groups that tend Brighid's sacred flame, keeping watch over a fire on their personal altars for one day out of a twenty day cycle before the fire is passed on in person or by intention to the next devotee in the rotation. On the twentieth day, Brighid is said to tend the flame Herself.

Some groups or orders may have initiatory rites, such as warrior-band initiations, or vision-seeking rites as part of the training and initiation of *filí* (poets) or *fáithe* (seers), where vigils in wild and sacred places might be performed for several days in a row.

Divination can be a part of ritual for many people, and divination is almost always done after making offerings, to determine if the offerings were found acceptable by the Deities or spirits. *Ogham* is commonly used for this, as is taking omens from the signs around us in nature such as by cloud-watching. There are also divinatory and trance rituals like the *tarbhfeis* (bull-feast), or the *teach an allais* (Gaelic sweat house) rites that different groups and individuals are attempting to reconstruct from details in the tales, manuscripts and folklore.

See also
✧ What is this Ogham stuff you keep mentioning? (p. 57)

Do you have to be a priest or a priestess to do a ritual?

No. Anyone can set up an altar for their Deities, their ancestors, and for the land spirits that dwell in their region. Anyone can pour out libation offerings to the Deities and the spirits, or make biodegradable food offerings at the base of a tree, into the fire, or in any other place that feels sacred to them and connected to the spirits of place.

Larger public rituals are usually best run by those with experience, but anyone can do personal daily rituals to show their respect for the sacred and to connect themselves to it.

What do you do for Samhain?

If you live in a place where it gets cold in the autumn, Samhain (*Oíche Shamhna*) tends to come at about the time of the first frost. (The calendar date is October 31st, but most CRs take this as an approximation rather than an exact date, and adjust the date to suit their regional climate.) In North America, pumpkins are ripe and the berries of hawthorns are red and getting soft. The festival itself is one of honoring the dead and of mourning the newly dead who have passed away in the just-finished year. Due to Her association with the dead, and *Oíche Shamhna* being the time of her mating with the Dagda, many CRs pay particular attention to the Morrígan at this festival.

It's appropriate to do a *saining* of the home with juniper – a New Year tradition in the highlands of Scotland – and to set up altars or shrines for the ancestors. On the night of *Oíche Shamhna*, many of us hold a feast with our friends and family where we invite the honored dead to come and feast with us. A place of honor is laid at the table or on the altar, where the first food of the feast and cups full of drink are placed for the dead. This portion of the food is never eaten by the living, but is instead offered outside when the feast is done. Candles are often lit for the dead, and their names are spoken. Tales about their lives are shared and toasts might be made in their names.

Divination is another common feature of this festival, and readings are often done to get a feel for the luck of the coming year. These might be divinations or readings done for individuals, or for a group or family as a whole. *Oíche Shamhna* is also the traditional start of the storytelling season, and traditional tales might be shared around the fire or after the feast while divination goes on in another room. As a time when the spirit-worlds are close at hand, ghost stories are fun and seasonal, as well as stories from our family or community histories. Music and dancing are common parts of modern *Oíche Shamhna* celebrations as well.

It is traditional in many Scottish and Irish communities for the teenagers to have a bonfire party on *Oíche Shamhna*, much as the younger children may attend more supervised parties or participate in trick-or-treating, which has its roots in some Gaelic guisers' customs. A number of traditional forms of divination have survived in children's games, and these are often a part of *Oíche*

Shamhna parties. One of these is the Gaelic tradition of divination by apple peel, where the apple is peeled in one long strip, and then the peel thrown over one's shoulder with all due ceremony; the peel is then supposed to form the first initial of the name of one's future spouse, or the first letter of the answer to one's question. Another divination game involves naming two nuts after two people, then putting them on the fire. Omens are taken from how the nuts roast or pop, and whether they move closer together or further apart.

As an agricultural and herding turning point, cattle were brought down from the mountains at this time and driven between two fires to purify and protect them for the winter. Excess animals were culled and sacrifice was performed, with the meat being prepared for winter storage. These days such things are rarely necessary unless you live rurally and raise your own animals for meat, but this would be a sensible time for slaughter and sacrifice, offering some portion to the Deities, ancestors and spirits as you put food away for yourself and the living family.

After this time, berries on the bush were traditionally considered the property of the spirits and no longer good for human consumption. The last grain that went unharvested was left in the field for the spirits as well.

See also

✧ Is it Samhain, Samhuinn or Samain? Why all these different spellings? (p. 58)
✧ Offerings seem to be a really important part of all these rituals. How do I make offerings? (p. 107)
✧ Do you Sacrifice animals? If so, why? (p. 112)

What do you do for Imbolc?

If you live in a climate where the winter is a time of snow and frozen ground, Imbolc (*Lá Fhéile Bríde*) is usually seen as the time of first thaw. Generally, some time between late January and late February, there is a time when the temperatures rise and the weather is briefly spring-like. Though there may still be snow on the ground, the first stirrings of spring can be felt.

In warmer climes, such as much of Ireland itself, the festival is marked by the first appearance of greenery, or the arrival of spring flowers such as primroses, crocuses or dandelions, which are sacred to Bríde. Scottish legend has it that on the day of

Brìghde, the snakes will emerge from the ground. This only makes sense if *Là Fhèill Brìghde* is celebrated at the true beginning of Spring but, given the climate in much of Scotland, perhaps the reference is more symbolic of Brìghde's connection with serpents, and the wisdom, healing and immortality they symbolize. This tradition of looking to the emergence of a hibernating animal to predict the weather has been Americanized as Groundhog Day.

A Scottish rhyme about Imbolc runs:

> *Candlemas Day, gin ye be fair,*
> *The half o' winter's to come and mair,*
> *Candlemas Day, gin ye be foul,*
> *The half o' winter's gane at Yule.*

Another version is:

> *Gin Candlemas be fair and clear,*
> *There'll be twa winters in the year.*
> (McNeill, F. Marian, *The Silver Bough*, Vol. Two. p. 30)

One legend has it that *Là Fhèill Brìghde* is the day the Cailleach gathers Her firewood for the rest of the winter. If She needs lots of firewood for the long winter to come, She will make the day clear and sunny. She can sometimes be seen on a clear *Là Fhèill Brìghde*, in the form of a large bird (often a crane or heron) carrying sticks in Her beak. Sighting the Cailleach is usually an omen of fierce, spring snowstorms to come. However, if She has decided to make the winter short this year, there is no reason for gathering wood; She can sleep all day and make the weather on *Là Fhèill Brìghde* as horrible as She wants.

It is still debatable whether the weather on *Lá Fhéile Bríde/Là Fhèill Brìghde* truly determines the weather for the rest of the season. Some CRs secretly think that the omen of a shorter winter is a hoped-for consolation prize for terrible weather on the festival day. Some feel gentle snow on Bríde's day is a good omen, much as is gentle rain on *Lá Lúnasa*.

Other forms of divination are practiced at *Là Fhèill Brìghde* as well. In Scotland, children have been known to chase crows on the festival day. The direction in which the crow flies is seen to signify the direction in which one's future spouse resides, and where one's future home will be.

Traditionally, Bríde is believed to wander the earth on the eve of *Lá Fhéile Bríde*, and many will leave an article of clothing or tool outside their door in hopes that Bríde will bless it for them as She passes by. In the morning, the ground is observed for signs of Her footprints.

Many CRs celebrate *Lá Fhéile Bríde* by welcoming Bríde into the house, based upon traditional rituals recorded in Ireland and Scotland by authors like Alexander Carmichael, F. Marian McNeill and Kevin Danaher. A favorite activity, especially for those with children, is to weave Bríde's Crosses out of rushes, straw, or yarn and sacred woods like rowan or willow, which are then blessed and hung in the house to provide protection for the following year. In Scotland, Imbolc is very much a holiday for girls, with the girl children dressing up in white, or festive, spring colors, and carrying an effigy of Brìghde through the community. This party will then stop at various houses for refreshments and maybe to offer a song or skit. If the weather is warm, sometimes the teenagers will have a bonfire party that night while the adults celebrate indoors.

As Bríde is a Goddess of holy wells, some CRs will center their *Lá Fhéile Bríde* ritual around asking Her blessings upon their local water source, making a pilgrimage to their well or reservoir and making offerings to Bríde. These offerings can include food and drink, as well as songs and poetry. Priestesses and priests of Bríde often take this time to do deep trancework with Her, and to divine Her wishes for the coming year.

Lá Fhéile Bríde is a very appropriate time to dedicate to writing or performing poetry in general, especially praise-poetry for Bríde and other liturgy. Whereas most of the other festivals involve travel and feasting with large groups of friends and extended family, *Lá Fhéile Bríde* is often the festival which focuses the most on the hearth and home, and quiet activities with one's household or local community.

See also

✦ Is it Samhain, Samhuinn or Samain? Why all these different spellings? (p. 58)

What do you do for Bealtaine?

In a climate with cold winters, this is the festival when spring turns to summer. (The calendar date is May 1st, though most CRs adjust this to suit their own climate.) CRs who have thorn trees locally often use their blossoming to mark the beginning of the light half of the year. Because Beltaine (*Lá Bealtaine*) is so linked with Samhain (*Oíche Shamhna*), many of the traditional activities that began then would end at this time. It is, for instance, the traditional end of the season of storytelling that began with *Oíche Shamhna*. Like *Oíche Shamhna*, it is also a time when the spirit world is seen to be particularly close at hand.

As this day is regarded as the beginning of summer in Scotland and Ireland, summer activities traditionally begin at this time. In herding communities, cattle and other livestock were moved from the byres and cottages to the summer pastures in the hills, and would be herded between two fires to purify them for the summer's coming. Many CRs still celebrate this custom by passing themselves and their pets, and livestock if they have any, between two fires on this holy day - whether the fires in question are bonfires, torches or candles.

Before leaving for the festival, it was traditional to douse all the fires in the village and clean out the hearth. In many households, this might be the only day of the year the fire was allowed to go out completely. The festival fires were then traditionally started by friction (a needfire or *tine-éigean*), and then tended through the festival and over the next night. This took place in areas such as Arran in Scotland and on many of the sacred hills in Ireland.

Flames from these bonfires were then taken home to relight the fires in each family hearth. Today, community bonfires can be built and vigils held on *Lá Bealtaine* eve before the people and animals pass through them at the dawning of the day, and candles lit from these fires can be brought home from the festival for good luck and protection. The bonfires are still regarded as a source of protection, good luck and fertility, though one should never give another fire from their own hearth – or anything else from the home – on this day, as the luck of the house would go with it. This is the one exception to the tradition of hospitality that was highly prioritized during all the rest of the year.

Some CRs also enact the custom of dousing and relighting the home fires by shutting off the pilot lights in their stoves and furnaces before they leave for the festival and upon their return relighting the pilot light with the flame from the festival fire. (If you do this, make sure you also know how to shut off the gas line, to make sure the renewed fire upon your return is not an explosion!) A practical way of carrying home the *Lá Bealtaine* flames is in a jar candle, camping-style candle lantern, or other shielded flame.

While the blooming of hawthorn marks the advent of *Lá Bealtaine*, it was considered unlucky to cut anything from thorn trees or to bring any part of them into the house except on *Lá Bealtaine* for fear of offending the *Aos Sí*. Seasonal altars are often decorated with blooming thorn this day because, for most, it is the one time of the year when it is not considered ill luck to cut the tree.

Holy wells are frequently visited on *Lá Bealtaine*. Well-veneration is a custom that still survives in the Celtic lands, and is believed to be a holdover from pre-Christian times. Many of these wells in Celtic lands have (or once had) thorn trees growing beside them. The well is traditionally approached before dawn and circled three times sunwise, while uttering prayers for health, prosperity, and healing. After these prayers are made, clooties (strips of cloth, often torn from the clothing of the one making the prayer) are tied to the branches of the tree, or a silver coin tossed into the well, to bring about the good wishes.

Traditionally in Scotland, a *Lá Bealtaine* bannock was made with oats, milk and eggs, mixed by hand and touched by no steel. One piece of the bannock was darkened with charcoal and whoever received this piece then had to pass three times over the bonfire to carry away any ill luck that might befall the community. Early greens might be picked as part of the ritual meal, to celebrate their return which would have been even more important in times when fresh greens were simply unavailable in winter. Some CRs choose not to eat bread or other baked goods for this ritual as a memory that grain might be scarce at this time of year.

Rowan equal-armed crosses were made and hung over cattle byres to protect them from the *Aos Sí* and other spirits who were abroad at this time, as the passage between worlds is easier on *Lá Bealtaine*, much as it also is at *Oíche Shamhna*. Water from holy wells was, and still is, sprinkled on people and animals to bless them.

At dawn on *Lá Bealtaine*, young women would gather dew and wash their faces with it to bring beauty and youth. The first water drawn from a well was additionally believed to have the power to bring healing and maintain one's youth.

Unlike most of the Neopagan community, CRs don't celebrate *Lá Bealtaine* with Maypoles. This tradition isn't Celtic, but was imported to the urban areas of Wales, Scotland and Ireland at a fairly late date from England, and never reached the more rural areas. A tradition practiced in Scotland and Ireland that has even found its way to Newfoundland is of decorating a May Bush, and often fierce competitions were held to see who could produce the most festive one. This was a way of celebrating the greening of the foliage, and the sign that life was returning to the land. This custom seems to have survived in an altered form in parts of the Irish and Scottish diaspora, most noticeably the Northeastern US, in the tradition of decorating trees with hanging "Easter Eggs" and other spring symbols at the beginning of spring.

See also

✦ Is it Samhain, Samhuinn or Samain? Why all these different spellings? (p. 58)

What do you do for Lúnasa?

In the US, some CRs celebrate berry season as a Lúnasa (*Lá Lúnasa*) or Tailltiu rite, around the beginning to the middle of August (depending on the weather each year) when the berries are finally ripening. In the Pacific Northwest, the festival is marked by the ripening of the blackberries, while in the Northeast, blueberries are usually the festival fruit.

The chosen day or weekend is spent going out to pick wild berries then having a feast where each dish contains berries in some form – berry vinegar in the salad dressing, berry sauce on salmon or chicken as a main dish, and berry pies or muffins for dessert. Berry offerings are given to the Deities and land spirits. Berry jam and pie fillings are made and preserved, berry vinegar is started, and sometimes berry wine as well. This fits in well with the *Lá Lúnasa* traditions of Ireland and Scotland, where berrying was part of the seasonal festival. It's a great communal activity that can involve an entire extended family from the youngest children to the elders, as well as any interested friends and neighbors. It also lives out a regional connection to the land as a local calendar point.

Lá Lúnasa/Tailltiu is also hurricane season in some areas. Some CRs on the east coast of the US include offerings of first fruits, favorite foods and poetry to the Cailleachan (Storm Hags) or Lugh, asking Them to please spare our homes, crops and loved ones from the late-summer storms. Gentle rain on the day of the festival is traditionally seen as Lugh's presence, and a good omen. Similarly, gentle winds, or high winds that manage to announce their presence without harming anyone, are seen as the presence of the boisterous Cailleachan. Other CRs feel that no wind at all on the festival is an even better omen, as it means the Cailleachan are busy elsewhere and too preoccupied to accidentally destroy the ripening crops.

Among the ancient Celts, this was a time of major assemblies, when rural peoples would journey to gather with distant neighbors for trade and celebration. This has survived in some families as the tradition of holding family reunions in August, or using this time for traveling to visit distant relatives. However, given the constraints of modern work schedules, especially among those who no longer farm, the reunions have in some cases been moved to a more convenient summer holiday, such as (in the US) the Fourth of July weekend.

Other traditions practiced by the ancient Celts at this festival included horse races, especially races in which the horses would swim some of the distance raced. It was also the time when the lambs were weaned from their dams, a custom which was suppressed in many (but not all) areas under Christianity due to its pagan associations, and replaced by different methods of weaning. Another common custom related to the time was the contracting of "temporary" marriages, which could be dissolved at will until the following *Lá Bealtaine*. Further, the festival as a whole was a time of significant sexual competitiveness among women (and possibly men), with much trickery recorded (such as one instance where a woman hired a clown to publicly tear the wig off of a rival at the Tailltiu fair). Among CRs, *Lá Lúnasa* begins the preferred wedding season, which lasts through to *Oíche Shamhna*.

See also
✧ Is it Samhain, Samhuinn or Samain? Why all these different spellings? (p. 58)

You talk a lot about these "practices," but can you describe them in more detail?

In CR, spiritual practices vary among different groups and individuals, but the common thread is that they are based on the Celtic lore and upon our best interpretations of how we can apply traditional methods of ritual, meditation, prayer, divination and other devotional acts to our daily lives. Different people take different paths on the road to spiritual development. The spiritual practices of some CRs are focused very much on the contemplative, the mystical, while others pursue a path based more on outward activity. Some prefer to work mostly alone, while others find their calling in community celebrations. Many endeavour to discover or develop a personal path that balances these approaches.

Folks walking the warrior path often find that martial arts practice is a meditation for them, and devote a part of their workout space to an altar to the Deities of combat and weaponry. Some might also study arts like blacksmithing or the making of bows and arrows as a part of their devotion. For some, horsemanship also comes into it, and their work with the animals is a part of their spiritual practice. Work with dogs and hunting may also play a part for some people, especially if they identify as Outsider/*fianna*. Many on the warrior path may also see working or volunteering in law enforcement, fire and rescue, emergency medical services, search and rescue and other similar services as an expression of their spirituality.

For those who follow a healer's path, the growing and preparation of healing herbs is often a part of spiritual practice. Prayers and offerings are made at planting and harvesting, and tending the growing plants is in itself an act of worship and meditation. Whether the herbs are grown in fields or window planters, the connection with the land and the spirits of nature offers a satisfying way of devotion to healing Deities, especially Goddesses like Brighid and Airmid.

CRs in general are encouraged to get outdoors and be in contact with the natural world. Those of us who live in cities will often go camping or go out for day hikes to meditate in wild places. We find that such practices recharge our emotional and spiritual resources, bringing us into deeper contact with the Deities and particularly with the spirits of the land. In places where camping and fires are allowed, offerings are often given to the sprits and Deities via the fire, vigils are held and prayers are made. Pilgrimages to the sea are not uncommon for those living further inland, especially if there is a connection to sea Deities like Manannán mac Lír or Fand, and offerings of food, flowers or drink are often placed in the water or poured out into the sea for Them.

The *filí* (poets) of Ireland postulated an energy structure in the body, consisting of three internal "cauldrons." These cauldrons were *Coire Goiriath* – the Cauldron of Warming, *Coire Érmai* – the Cauldron of Motion, and *Coire Sofhis* – the Cauldron of Wisdom. Many folk who are working on modern *filidecht* in an Irish or Scottish CR tradition find this a useful model for meditation and healing work. Further information about a CR perspective on this material can be found in Erynn Rowan Laurie's *"Cauldron of Poesy"*[15] article. It includes a preliminary translation of the text, commentary, and ideas for breathing exercises as well as thoughts on the path of CR *filidecht*. An edition of the text in Irish, along with a later, more complete translation in English by Laurie is also available.[16]

Many of us do divinatory work, usually with *ogham*, an early Irish alphabet. Divination or omen-taking is often a part of larger rituals and the making of offerings, so that we can get some sense of the attitude of the Deities, ancestors or nature spirits toward the work that we've done. The study of *ogham* divination and other omen-taking practices forms and informs many of our approaches. Dreamwork and the cultivation of vision are also an important part of personal practice for many of those on the more mystical end of CR.

Almost anything in a person's daily life can be ritualized and surrounded with the sacred. Preparation of meals can be a sacred task. Cleaning the house can be approached as both a meditation

---

[15] *http://www.seanet.com/~inisglas/cauldronpoesy.html*
[16] *http://www.seanet.com/~inisglas/cop1.html*

and a spiritual cleansing – a physical and spiritual act of *glanadh* ("cleaning, clearance"). Welcoming a guest with food and drink is practicing the sacred act of hospitality, and is a concrete example of virtue in action. Study of history and lore is a devotional act to Deities of knowledge, eloquence and wisdom, like Ogma and Brighid.

Spiritual practice is not limited to things set apart from daily life. Daily life *is* a spiritual practice.

See also

✧ How do you create sacred space? (p. 93)
✧ What is this Ogham stuff you keep mentioning? (p. 57)
✧ What can I do to get started? (p. 137)
✧ Offerings seem to be a really important part of all these rituals. How do I make offerings? (p. 107)
✧ You talk a lot about the role of the Outsiders. What do you mean by that? (p. 91)
✧ I've read about Cú Chulainn's training with Scáthach. What is this "Salmon Leap" or the "sword feat"? Is there a Celtic Martial Art form? (p. 44)

Offerings seem to be a really important part of all those rituals. How do I make offerings?

Offerings are a very important part of CR practice. They are made on all the major ritual occasions, and are frequently made in small, private rituals as well. Some people make daily or weekly offerings to their house spirits, ancestors or Deities as a regular part of their devotional practices.

Making offerings is a very simple thing on the outside. It would seem to be just a matter of placing food and drink on an altar, or leaving these things in an outdoor location that you consider sacred or connected to Deities, ancestors or land spirits. In truth, it's a more complicated thing and involves both energy and intent. Offerings are not just food or drink, but can also be creative works that you've made, or performance of poetry, music, or other arts. Sometimes candles or incense are lit as a part of the offering. Food and drink, though, are the most often used items, and are most consistently available to anyone in any region.

Traditional food offerings include milk, butter, mead or ale, baked goods, oats, hazelnuts, rowan berries, apples, and other items frequently mentioned in the tales and lore. Meat may also be part of an offering, and salmon is frequently given as an offering by those seeking wisdom. Water is also a common offering, particularly if it is water from a sacred spring or holy well that was collected ritually during a pilgrimage to a sacred site. When offering to the local land spirits, some people practicing CR in North America may also include offerings of tobacco, maize, sage, or other native food or plant items, depending on the traditional likes and dislikes of these spirits and what they seem to be requesting of us.

When preparing the offering, it's good to offer prayers to the Deities and spirits that you'll be giving it to. This helps you focus your attention on Them and on the sacred intent of the creation of an offering. A ritual cleansing or *saining* of the people and the items involved in the offering is often done in preparation for making offerings. Food and drink can be placed in a vessel used primarily or only for making offerings. It doesn't have to be anything fancy or expensive, but it should be something that you consider beautiful as well as functional. For offerings into fire, the food and drink will be put in the flames, but the vessels would be kept unless you place the offerings in wooden vessels that you intend as part of the offering or sacrifice. Offerings made outdoors don't have to be left on plates or in containers. Liquid offerings are usually poured out as prayers are offered. Outdoor offerings should be given to the earth or placed in the water with care, however, just as offerings made indoors are placed on the altar with care. Offerings are never to be simply tossed on the ground like trash.

The offering of alcoholic drinks is somewhat controversial. It is clear from the Celtic lore that many Deities and spirits may appreciate offerings of mead or ale. However, those of us in living in the Americas are conscious of the fact that many First Nations peoples feel it is taboo to pour alcohol onto the earth, as it is seen as a poison. A compromise found by those who still choose to offer alcohol is to only offer it when it can be poured into flames and consumed by the fire.

The actual making of the offering should be accompanied by prayer or poetry dedicated to the Deities or spirits. The words don't have to be fancy, but should be from the heart. Some people like to make their offering prayers in Gaelic or the language of their Deities, while others speak the prayers in their own native languages. For some folks, it's important to make offerings with traditional words or a similar verbal formula each time, and they may compose offertory prayers that are used each time an offering is made. Others find it more appropriate to make each offering with words inspired in the moment and specific to the purpose of each individual offering.

The attention of everyone present during the offerings should be fixed on the task at hand, without side chatter going on. Offerings are a vital part of our social and spiritual contracts with the Deities, the ancestors and the spirits. To make an offering is to extend hospitality to those entities, to open ourselves up to communication with them, and should always be done with reverence and respect. Offerings may be made in thanks for services that the Deities and spirits have given, or as a regular part of your daily or weekly practice. They may be made as part of a larger ritual, or as special requests for assistance and favor in times of need. When making offerings as part of a request, remember also to make offerings in thanks when that request is granted.

Offerings indoors on your altar might be left overnight or for a few hours, but should then be taken outside and given to the land whenever possible. Offerings to the Deities and spirits should not be eaten afterwards. CR belief has generally been that the *toradh* ("substance") of ritually offered food and drink has been consumed by the spirits, and that to consume that which was given to the Deities and spirits is subtly harmful to the living. This was also a part of early Scottish and Irish belief and, due to this, offerings left at the doorstep were usually watched to see that the family cats and dogs didn't get into them. If you have a fireplace, woodstove, or other place to make a fire, it's also quite acceptable to burn the offerings after they're removed from the altar.

In cases where offerings are made at large public rituals in urban settings, it may not be practical to put the offerings outside immediately afterwards, for health and safety reasons. Leaving offerings in the alley behind a building will feed the rats and not make your neighbors happy. In cases like this, food and drink can either be kept temporarily in a storage container and later placed in a park or in a flowing stream, or – with proper acknowledgement and prayers – it might need to be disposed of in a dumpster.

That option, however, is a last resort and should only be done when there is no chance of taking the offerings to leave them in a natural setting. Bearing this in mind, when planning an urban, indoor ritual, most CRs will make sure that a trip to the park afterwards, at least for the officiating clergy, is incorporated into the schedule.

After offerings are made, many CRs do divination to see if the offerings were accepted. This may involve taking an omen from the surroundings, or drawing an *ogham fiodh* to gauge the response of the Deities and spirits. If the omen or divination is unfavorable, it is wise to consider making other offerings and refocusing your intent. In this way, offerings are a time not only for speaking to the Deities and spirits, but also for listening to Their messages to us.

See also

✧ What is this Ogham stuff you keep mentioning? (p. 57)

Chapter Seven

Ethics

What is the ethical basis of CR?

CR ethics are grounded in traditional Celtic virtues which should be embraced, adopted, and integrated into one's daily life. This approach is known as a "virtue theoretic ethical system," as it sets forth multiple positive guidelines for behaviour – "thou shalt"s rather than a series of "thou shalt not"s.

We believe in hospitality, truth, generosity, taking care of each other, wisdom, knowledge, eloquence, mercy, justice, and the duty of the strong to support the weak rather than prey upon them. No one is without innate worth, and treating others with respect is emphasized. Because we're human, we don't always live up to our ideals, but we feel it's a more positive approach than enumerating a list of things that are forbidden. For a more in-depth look at ways that CR approaches ethics, *"The Truth Against the World: Ethics and Modern Celtic Paganism"*[17] offers one view of the way ethics are treated within CR today.

Some CR's subscribe to a set of virtues similar to the Nine Noble Virtues of Ásatrú. A common set of virtues followed by many emphasizes Truth, Honor, Justice, Loyalty, Courage, Community, Hospitality, Strength, and Gentleness. Other ancient texts offer guidelines for leadership and adages of everyday wisdom. Such sources include *The Instructions of Cormac*, the Irish Triads, the *Audacht Morainn*, and many others.

---

[17] *http://www.seanet.com/~inisglas/ethics.html*

Warriors are honored in most forms of CR, but violence is not their first or the most obvious solution to the great majority of problems. Individuals within CR may be military or veterans, or they may be peace activists. In many cases, they are both, and many others are part of a wide spectrum between. The place of the warrior is seen as a legitimate protector of the tribe, rather than indulging in first strikes against those who have done no harm.

CR firmly and absolutely rejects racism, sexism, homophobia and other forms of discrimination which divide people into warring camps.

Do you sacrifice animals? If so, why?

While most CRs do not practice animal sacrifice, a small number do. Most CRs live in urban areas, which makes such a practice impractical. Many do not feel any need to sacrifice animals, instead offering other things to the Deities and spirits. Examples include jewelry and other fine metalwork offered to bodies of water, libations, poetic efforts, or fruits and vegetables – as you can see, there is some overlap between the concepts of offering and sacrifice. Carnivorous CRs may take a moment to thank the spirit of the animal that gave its life for our nourishment, but the actual killing of animals for sustenance is not part of urban life.

Sacrifice is never undertaken lightly by those who do it, and it is done to provide food as well as for theological reasons. No one in CR is compelled to take part in sacrificial rites if it makes them uncomfortable. No animals are sacrificed that are not used for food, so there is no need to be concerned that neighborhood pets are going to wind up on anyone's sacrificial altar. The most common animals offered in sacrifice and consumed are chickens, pigs, sheep, cattle, goats, or other livestock whose flesh you can buy perfectly legally at your local grocery store.

The few who do practice animal sacrifice are living in rural areas and have made a choice to grow and raise some of their own food, including meat. This is not done just so they can make sacrifices, but rather because of their dislike of the current manner in which most livestock is raised. Sacrifice is sharing the life essence with the Deities and spirits – the blood and often a prime portion of the meat, or one of the animals if small, are offered to Them in thanks for Their gifts to us. It is a natural part of the process of life and death, just as one who makes art might offer their skills to the Goddesses and Gods. Although few CRs are in a position to raise cattle today, many of those who raise smaller livestock still follow the idea of killing the non-breeding food animals at *Oíche Shamhna* (November eve).

It should also be noted that other religions, like Judaism, Islam, and the Afro-Diasporic traditions such as Santería, have practices that are sacrificial in nature. Animals that are slaughtered under Kosher or Halal laws are part of a practice that is protected by US law, and the practice of animal sacrifice was also declared legal as a matter of religious freedom in the US Supreme Court case, **Church of the Lukumi Babalu Aye v. City of Hialeah (1993).**[18]

See also

✧ Offerings seem to be a really important part of all those rituals. How do I make offerings? (p. 107)

✧ You talk a lot about these "practices," but can you describe them in more detail? (p. 105)

The Celts were headhunters and performed human sacrifices. Why would anyone want to go back to that?

Quite simply, we don't. One of the purposes of CR is to rediscover the things of value in the early Celtic cultures, such as the spiritual elements that were lost when polytheism was replaced by Christianity. While there may be religious and cultural elements that we wish to bring forward into our modern lives, we are not an historical re-enactment group. We are generally law-abiding modern people and enjoy things like indoor plumbing, central heating, modern medicine, and eyeglasses. What we want to do is bring forward those things that are of value and work with what is relevant for the time in which we live.

See also

✧ How do you decide what aspects of Celtic culture to keep and what to discard? (p. 52)

✧ Are you guys like the SCA? (p. 123)

---

[18] *http://atheism.about.com/library/decisions/religion/bl_l_LukumiHialeah.htm*

You say CR is "pro-queer," but is this traditional?

While there are no sweeping statements promoting homosexuality in the ancient Celtic lore, there are multiple accounts from external observers who commented on the widespread practice of homosexuality among the Gaulish Celts. The Greek philosopher Posidonius, who traveled into Gaul to investigate the truth of the stories told about the Celtic tribes, put it rather bluntly: "The Gaulish men prefer to have sex with each other." This is supported by some Aristotelian commentaries as well.

As far as we know, the ancient Celts had no laws or known prohibitions against homosexual behaviour. To the contrary, there are tales and histories in which homosexuality is mentioned in a rather matter-of-fact way, as well as many other accounts which, while containing no explicit mention of any character's sexual orientation, celebrate deep bonds between persons of the same gender. Roman and Greek accounts both mention Celtic warriors who were deeply insulted if their offers of homosexual sex were refused.

There is at least one Irish tale, "Niall Frossach" from *The Book of Leinster*, where lesbian sex is specifically mentioned (as "playful mating"), and no one in the tale treats this as remarkable or shameful. The myths and histories contain references to Islands of Women and societies of "virgin" priestesses, and there are a number of Deities who do not fit neatly into rigid gender roles. There are Goddesses of war and battle, and Gods of love and poetry. The Sea God Manannán is the only God welcome on the Isle of Women, and he drives his chariot through fields of purple flowers. There is also a tradition of male praise-poets who wrote about the kings they served as a lover writes of their beloved. Many historical commentaries on warriors and monastics speak of devoted companions who shared a bed, and often the love between these companions is celebrated in poetry and songs.

While most scholars believe that "Gay identity" is a modern construct, and only exists in reaction to oppression, there is also agreement that homosexuality and bisexuality have always existed, and were certainly a part of Celtic culture.

As CR is about adapting ancient tradition to modern life, even if suddenly someone discovered an ancient Celtic tale that seemed to portray homophobia, it is highly doubtful that any of us would consider changing our personal views on that basis. If it ever turns out that there was homophobia among our ancestors, it would be no more worth preserving than slavery.

See also

✧ I hear you're just a political movement. (p. 65)

Do you do magic? If so, what kind and why?

While magic in and of itself is not particularly emphasized in CR, it is a part of many CRs' lives. Generally it is seen as an integral part of daily life rather than a specific set of techniques separated from our daily and spiritual lives. Traditionally, magic was done for both helpful, healing purposes, and to call down ill-luck and destruction upon rivals or enemies. Druids are described as doing battle magic, and the God Lugh performed cursing magic called *córrguineacht* or Crane-magic as part of the great battle of Magh Tuiredh.

CR ethics do not forbid the use of magic, whether positive or negative, though it is apparent when looking at the lore that negative magic often had negative consequences. In the Irish laws regarding poets, the process for performing the *Glam Dícenn*, a great curse, is described. Leaving aside the fact that the performance of this curse would be essentially impossible today for a variety of reasons, it was noted that if the curse was laid unjustly, rather than the earth opening up and swallowing the one cursed (along with his livestock and family), the cursing *file* (poet) and her or his assistants would be swallowed up instead.

Generally speaking, magic was fairly simple and almost always involved the use of poetry or song. Magic-infused ritual was involved in the harvest of healing herbs, and healing magic was accompanied by spoken poetic charms as well. CRs, like most modern Pagans, sometimes do magic for wealth and good luck, to help find jobs, or to protect our homes, families and property. Magic is so deeply entwined with the worship of Deity that it is sometimes difficult to distinguish a difference between religious ritual, prayer and acts of magic. However, there is nothing in CR which requires a belief in the effectiveness of magic in an objective sense, nor is there any requirement to practice it.

In modern Gaelic-based CR, *ogham* is often used as a vehicle for magic and divination. Though the *ogham* letters themselves probably do not date back to pre-Christian times, many find *ogham* to be a useful system for organizing older ideas and symbolic associations, and the lore speaks of the druids using it for various purposes. In this spirit, many of us feel it is proper for us to work with *ogham* as a modern magical and divinatory system. Many approaches are taken to the material, but most CRs who have taken up a study of *ogham* say they've found it useful.

When we practice magic of any kind, we feel it is important to keep in mind the virtues of our path, and to work magic for beneficial rather than harmful ends. While we do not embrace the Wiccan Rede, we do have a positive set of ethics that guide our actions in both our everyday lives and our spiritual and magical work. Positive magical work, if you have an aptitude for magic, enhances reputation, and reputation is a very important part of our participation in community. In CR, we are judged as much by the way we conduct our magical lives as by what we do in community and within the spiritual context of our private worship.

See also

✧   What is this Ogham stuff you keep mentioning? (p. 57)

Chapter Eight

About Druids and Druidry

Are you a Druid?

Most practitioners of CR tend to avoid the word "druid" unless they are actively serving as priests or priestesses to a community of people. The word implies a great deal of knowledge and study that most folks just don't have yet and, quite frankly, some people aren't interested in being priests or priestesses. There are a lot of CR folk who are much more comfortable in the role of householder, homesteader, artisan or warrior, or some unique combination of these roles.

Those of us who do use the word "druid" to describe ourselves usually only do so after much soul-searching, many years of study and practice, and after other elders in the community acknowledge us as such. It is never a title taken out of the blue because we feel like it. CR is not in and of itself a form of modern "Druidism" or "Neo-druidism" though a number of CRs consider themselves to be on a druidic path, and working towards being worthy of the title. The acknowledgement of this title (*draoí* in Irish) usually comes only after many years of contributing substantially to the local and online CR communities.

Anyone presenting themselves to a CR group or individual who claims this title is likely to be quizzed on their knowledge and experience rather than being taken at face value. This is not meant as an insult, it is simply that we hold the title in high regard and believe that only those qualified should bear it. Anyone can call themselves a druid, but few genuinely live up to the claim. Furthermore, such quizzes of knowledge are attested in the literature as having occurred between druids, so if there is a problem with it, blame the Celts.

See also
✦ What's the difference between a warrior path and a poet's path? Are there other options within CR? (p. 43)

Aren't all Druids men?

No. The tales and Classical commentators are quite clear and unanimous that there were both male and female druids. CR does not discriminate in regard to gender or sexual identity, and in fact many of the founders of CR are gay, bi, lesbian, or transfolk. Feminism is an important part of many CRs' lives. Anyone who chooses to dedicate their life to study and service to the community and who has a sincere calling from the Deities may eventually become a druid.

See also
✦ Are you a Druid?. (p. 117)

Since the Druids didn't write anything down, how do you know what you believe is accurate, and isn't just guessing?

See
✦ If they didn't write anything down, how do you know what they believed? (p. 29)

Weren't the Druids the Celtic Shamans?

The druids filled many functions in Celtic societies, only some of which involved mysticism, spirit-mediation, or other types of interactions with the Otherworld. More often, the "druids" were teachers, lawyers, historians and political advisors. Only some druids were spiritual officials or ritual leaders.

CR practitioners do not refer to themselves as shamans for a variety of reasons.

See also
✦ Do you practice Celtic shamanism? (p. 133)

Did the Celts really call their priests "Druids"?

Yes and no. They called their priests, priestesses, and other people who fulfilled an official religious role by a variety of titles, in the languages and dialects spoken in their particular time and region. "Druid" is an English translation of the Irish *draoí* and the equivalent from other Celtic cultures.

But the druids were also in large part the intellectual class in Celtic societies. "Druids" included doctors, lawyers, the equivalent of modern college professors, and other non-religious educated elites, both male and female. This is part of the reason why CRs are reluctant to take the title of druid upon themselves without a specific understanding of what is meant by it in the community they serve.

See also
✦ Are you a Druid? (p. 117)

Do you separate people into Bards, Ovates and Druids?

Generally speaking, no. These distinctions are most often used to indicate degrees of progress in Neo-druidic organizations like the Order of Bards, Ovates and Druids (or OBOD). The Neo-druidic groups who currently use this degree system are generally based on the assumptions of the 18th century "Druidic Revival," which tend to have a very different approach than what we are doing with CR. The Neo-druidic groups, especially the older ones, do not always have a Celtic orientation, nor do most of them prioritize scholarship.

When dealing with titles like bard, ovate, or druid, we have to remember that context is important. While in medieval Wales being called a bard was a mark of respect, in Ireland a bard was an untrained poet, and generally regarded as inferior to a *file*. Modern Scots Gaelic uses *bàrd* to refer to any poet today, and the word does not necessarily carry the musical connotation that it does in the minds of most modern Pagans. *Ovate* is a Brythonic word referring, most likely, to a variety of prophesier. It is related to *vate*, a word used by Caesar to describe some members of the class he called "druids," and to the Modern Irish word *fáidh* "prophet; wise man, sage." In Modern Irish, *ollamh* is a title used by the master of a craft, or by a professor at a university. Originally, it was used to refer to a master of a craft, but especially a master poet, or *file*. The issues surrounding the use of the title "druid" are addressed in several other questions in this FAQ. Due to all these concerns, there is currently no CR group that divides its members into the grades of bard, ovate or druid.

See also

✧ How do you determine who your spiritual elders are when you don't always have an ordered hierarchy? (p. 36)

✧ Are you a Druid? (p. 117)

Can you be a Druid even if you are not Irish/Welsh/etc.?

Anyone who has a sincere calling to be of service to the Celtic Deities and the CR community can study to become a druid. We do not discriminate in any way based on national, ethnic, or racial origins. The Deities call whom They will, and it's not our business to say which Gods and Goddesses you can follow based on the color of your skin or the percentage of your blood that hails from the Celtic lands, or anywhere else for that matter. Anyone discriminating based on these things is not practicing CR, despite any claims they may make to the contrary.

See also

✧ Don't you have to be Irish/Scottish/Welsh to be a Celtic Reconstructionist? (p. 27)

Aren't Druids sun worshippers, like Wiccans are moon worshippers?

No. This misconception seems to have originated with the 17th century antiquarians who first started Neo-"druidic" orders based on Masonic models. These romantic revivalists were not looking to Celtic history for their theology or cosmology, and instead chose to believe that all Gods are solar in nature, and that the druids practiced a form of monotheism that presaged Christianity. Actual Celtic scholarship proved these models false, but with so many people reading the books written in that era, these outdated misconceptions found their way into the occult community and are still repeated by those who do not actually study Celtic history.

Celtic religion does value the beauty and power of nature, and celebrates the changing of the seasons and the shifting balance of darkness and light. But while there are Deities who are described as bright or effulgent, and Who are connected to the changing seasons of the year, there is no Celtic Sun God. Many occult or Neopagan writers have claimed that Lugh is a Sun God; however the lore actually shows Him to be connected with lightning, storms, and rain. Ogma being called "Sun-Faced" is a reference to His brilliant wisdom and strength, not a solar affinity. All the words for the sun in the Celtic languages are female, and even in the case of Goddesses who have distinct solar attributes – such as Áine and Grian (Whose name literally means "sun") – to describe Them only as Sun Goddesses would be limiting and misleading.

The religion of the ancient Celts was not about sun worship, nor is CR.

A lady druid is a dryad, right?

No. A "dryad" is a Greek tree-spirit. It has nothing to do with druids.

This misconception, like so many others, seems to have begun with the fantasies of some of the eighteenth or early nineteenth century romantic revivalists, who were uninterested in cultural or historical accuracy. It has been repeated by some modern writers such as Barbara Walker who postulates, purely on the accidental resemblance of the words, an entire Greek female "druid" cultus. Whatever other virtues that the works of these writers might have, etymological rigor is clearly not one of them.

Chapter Nine

How is CR different from Wicca, Celtic Shamanism, etc.?

Are you guys like the SCA?

No. We are not interested in recreating the Iron Age. We don't call ourselves Lord or Lady or try to claim any royal or noble titles for ourselves. We're interested in the early Celtic cultures for what they can teach us about the spiritual nature of humanity, and in applying that in our very modern lives.

Those who follow a warrior path do so for the same reasons people study Eastern martial arts – to develop our bodies, minds and spirits within a particular philosophical framework.

Similarly, those who are reconstructing the path of the druid or *file*, or that of the CR householder (to name only a few examples) are finding the ways these ancient roles, and their associated practices, fulfill our current spiritual and emotional needs and the needs of our communities. We are seeking to integrate these findings into a modern life that is spirit-suffused and functional, rather than recreating an Iron Age context.

While some CR individuals may also participate in recreational groups such as The Society for Creative Anachronism (SCA) or renaissance faires, that is seen as a very separate and distinct part of their lives and not a part of their spirituality. CRs are no more or less drawn to historical re-enactment groups than are any other segment of the population.

So you're a Satanist?

No. CR doesn't have any Deity concept even vaguely equivalent to Satan. You can't worship what's not a part of your religion.

Many CRs don't view the spirits or Deities who may be unfriendly to us as "evil" but rather as a variety of "Outsiders." Perhaps these beings are hostile, perhaps just unfriendly and unknown, but they might also be spirits or Deities who are friendly to others. For example, many Irish Reconstructionists might consider the Fomorians adversaries of their Deities. However, for those following Tory Island traditions, Balor, a prominent Fomorian, was revered. This does not make the Tory Islanders a CR equivalent of "Satanists," by any means. They are simply people who live in a different place and have different alliances. Similarly, some CRs with a connection to the sea make offerings to Domnu, Who is seen as a primal Goddess of the deep, and Who also gives Her name to the tribe of the Fomorians, who are sometimes called the Túatha Dé Domnann. While the Fomorians might have had conflicts with the Túatha Dé Danann in particular tales, this enmity may only apply to that conflict; it does not make all the Fomorians inherently evil.

It is also clear that one can only generalize so far about the Fomorians, or any other beings who have at times been at conflict with other beings. The old tales are clear that some of the Túatha Dé Danann are part Fomorian, or were raised by Fomorian foster-parents. Like humans, spirits and Deities are not limited by their race or upbringing, and can change over time, especially if it is in their best interests to form new alliances and let go of old conflicts.

It is also clear in the lore that many Deities and spirits can act as tricksters. Even a Celtic Deity Who is usually helpful may decide to try and trick a human, either because They feel it's the best way for that human to learn a lesson, or because They are testing that person. Therefore, in CR, it is important to remember that we are expected to be strong and smart, and not be gullible. Just because some spirit may claim to be a Deity, or may even be a Deity, we don't agree to do things that go against our ethics simply because some being we perceive as wiser appears to be suggesting that we do so.

See also
✧ You talk a lot about the role of the Outsiders. What do you mean by that? (p. 91)

So you're Wiccan?

No. Wicca and CR have no real resemblance to each other. Rituals are not conducted in the same ways. The worldview is very different, as is our view of the Deities. Some branches of Wicca refer to themselves as "Celtic," but for the most part all they've done is borrow a few Deity and holiday names, neither using any of the early or modern Celtic forms of worship, nor the basic cosmology that is shown in the source texts and archaeological sites.

See also
✧ What is the difference between CR and Celtic Neo-Paganism? (p. 130)
✧ Why do CRs hate Wicca and Wiccans? (p. 77)
✧ Who can initiate me into your super-duper secret tradition handed down from the early mists of time? You are the "hidden children of the Goddess," right? (p. 70)

If there's no Rede you must not have any ethics.

The Wiccan Rede is just that – Wiccan. It has been widely accepted across many eclectic Neopagan traditions, but it is not the only model for ethical behavior, even within the larger Pagan community. It is certainly not a Celtic model for ethical behavior in any historical sense, nor do CRs adhere to it beyond the fact that it's usually a good idea to minimize the harm you do in the world.

Christianity doesn't follow the Rede, but it has its own ethical structures, as do Hinduism, Islam, Buddhism, and all the other religions of the world. CR ethics are based on the virtues illustrated in the tales, instruction texts like *The Instructions of Cormac*, the Triads of Ireland where they address ethical situations, and the Gaulish ideal that "the people should worship the Gods, do no evil, and exercise courage."

See also
✧ What is the ethical basis of CR? (p. 111)
✧ Do you do magic? If so, what kind and why? (p. 115)

So you worship the Triple Goddess, the Maiden/Mother/Crone?

The idea that all, or even **any**, Goddesses fit into a Maiden/Mother/Crone structure is not Celtic. Robert Graves made it up when he was writing his "work of poetic imagination," *The White Goddess*. Celtic Goddesses appear in the traditional lore as a variety of ages, in a variety of different guises, as it suits Their purposes. To the extent that They can be categorized at all, They are categorized by function, not age. They are seen as well-rounded individuals, with Their own preferences, relationships and activities, much like most of the humans you'll meet. That said, there are a number of Celtic Deities who are known to be threefold. Brighid and The Morrígan are two of the best-known, but they are usually described as three sisters, and not of radically different ages.

So you don't worship the Lord and Lady?

Again, we are polytheists. The idea that "all Goddesses are one Goddess" (or "all Gods are one God") comes from the early twentieth century British occultist, Dion Fortune, and from some of the ideas of late Hinduism. It is not a part of Celtic tradition.

See also
✧ Do you worship The Goddess? (p. 83)
✧ Which Gods do you worship? (p. 84)
✧ So you worship all the Celtic Deities? (p. 84)
✧ What do you mean when you say that it's not a dualistic religion? (p.90)

So you think God is a woman then? Isn't that what all that mumbo jumbo feminist witchcraft crap is about?

The Celtic ancestors worshipped both Goddesses and Gods. As polytheists, we believe the Divine takes a variety of appearances, and can manifest as any gender.

The Celts were basically a patriarchal society, and this is reflected in the lore. However, there is reason to believe that they placed more emphasis on the Goddesses than did the other Indo-European (IE) cultures. For instance, it has been noted that in other IE cultures, the line of derivation of Sovereignty is from the

Sky Father, while in Celtic societies it seems to derive from the local Land Goddess. This is not merely a cosmetic difference, but is rather a fundamental difference in philosophy. While they were far from being egalitarian in a modern sense, the ancient Celts were more egalitarian than most other IE-derived peoples, with some women owning property, fighting, and having more rights than women in other cultures of the time. It is also possible that some Celtic societies were matrilineal in structure, though this was probably not the norm.

Due to this patriarchal history, many CRs believe there has been too much focus on Gods in the past and that the Goddesses have been neglected. So they seek to rectify this in their personal practice. Others don't really think much about gender and simply focus on the Deities of whatever sort Who call to them. Either path is valid. Sometimes the Christian monks chose to record a great deal of information on a God, and a Goddess will be simply dismissed as that God's wife, mother, or daughter. Given this historical trend, there is sometimes more reconstruction work to do for Goddesses than there is for Gods. This process of reconstruction can involve weaving disparate threads from a variety of different manuscripts and tales until a more complete picture emerges. In other cases, such as Brighid or the Morrígan, we have a great deal of information on some of the Goddesses. This may be one of the things that contributes to Their ongoing popularity.

Do you cast the circle and call quarters in your rituals?

No. These ideas come from the late 19th century Ceremonial Magic conception of how to delineate and sanctify sacred space, and as such are based on some **very** questionable interpretations of books from the Medieval and Renaissance grimoire tradition, combined with ideas of no known provenance (but which seem likely to have derived from the imaginations of the people who created the 19th century Ceremonial Magic tradition). When Gardner created Wicca, he incorporated these ideas into the Wiccan ritual format. However, they are not part of Celtic tradition.

On the other hand...

It should be noted that there has been some recent vigorous debate regarding a similar issue within CR. One camp posits the validity of a system of directional attributes from a story called "The Settling of the Manor of Tara," in which the four or five directions, based on the provinces of Ireland, are attributed to certain broad concepts (like "wisdom" or "prosperity"), and the characters in the story are ritually seated in accord with their homelands and, by extension, those attributes. However, no one has tried to come up with cosmological/spatial associations for other texts that include similar "seating charts," including *Fled Bricrenn* and *Togail Bruidne Da Derga*, even though *Fled Bricrenn* has thirty-four seating sections, the exact same number of seating compartments that were found in the "forty-metre structure" at Emain Macha.

The other camp believes that the "Tara" arrangement holds little use for ritualistic activities, since it is little more than a seating chart in the story in question, it is only mentioned in that one story, and one could just as easily posit a system of thirty-four directions from these examples. They also feel that it is unrealistic to limit the qualities associated with entire areas of the country, and even less appropriate to then transfer these "directional" qualities to other diverse lands in the diaspora. This camp believes the Three Realms cosmology is more authentically Celtic – it is mentioned far more often in the lore, and ancient Celts swore their oaths by land, sea and sky. Adherents to the Three Realms system also tend to believe that the recent, limited popularity of the four (or five) directions structure is due to a desire among some for something that feels similar to Wicca, or that will appeal to those more familiar with Wicca and Wiccan-influenced traditions like most Eclectic Neopaganism. However, as CR was begun as an alternative to non-Celtic traditions such as Wicca, they see no reason for structures that cater to that desire. The Three Realms camp is the older one in the CR community.

We freely note that there is archaeological evidence of some ritual structures with four posts aligned with the compass points around a central post. However, other structural patterns also existed, and the mere existence of this structural pattern does not automatically mean that they used this to "invoke" the directions and the qualities they may or may not represent. It may reflect the five sacred trees that are noted elsewhere in the lore. For all we know, they may have considered those trees to be what supported the world. However, that last is supposition and barely qualifies as UPG. It could also simply mean that this was a convenient way of building any structure, be it for sacred or secular use.

There is evidence that, among some Celts, the winds (*gaoithe*) were associated with qualities or colors, as seen in the *Saltair na Rann* and some of the Irish and Scottish poetry. However, winds from many directions – generally twelve winds and sub-winds – were sometimes named, and even the "attributes" of the main four were based on local geography and seasonal weather patterns, not on any rigid, universal, nor "astral" conception of directional qualities. CRs who acknowledge the winds, or look to them for omens, usually follow this localized approach and so adapt the various traditional associations to their local environments.

Marian McNeill does include a brief mention of someone drawing a circle on the ground with a dirk or branch, as protection against "evil spirits," and with the utterance "The Cross of Christ be upon me!" However, this was recorded in fairly recent times, and there is no way of telling whether this was only a post-Christian practice, or based on something older. Nor is there any indication of how widespread this practice may have been, especially as McNeill seems to be the only mention of it. But even if this was based on some pre-Christian precedent, it does seem clear that it was seen only as a form of emergency protection from evil, not a standard ritual form, nor was it a way of interacting with beneficial spirits.

Though opinions on these bits of lore differ, all CRs do agree that the Ceremonial Magic and Wiccan concepts of "casting" a circle and "calling quarters," and the cosmological justifications thereof, are completely alien to the practices of any of the Celtic peoples. Since some persons who wish to further specific agendas have seized on these mild controversies as "proof" that Wicca is derived from Celtic traditions, or that Wiccan ritual forms can be used in CR, they deserve to be addressed here.

See also

⬦ Why don't you want me waving my knife at the spirits? (p. 130)
⬦ How do you create sacred space? (p. 93)

Why don't you want me waving my knife at the spirits?

The Insular Celtic lore is very clear that "cold iron" is offensive to the *Aos Sí*. As the *Aos Sí* are variously seen as the Goddesses and Gods, the ancestors, and/or the spirits of nature, it is a bad idea to anger them. The idea of walling out spirits and attempting to command them with knives and swords is derived from Ceremonial Magic, and the traditions influenced by it, like Wicca. However, CR is built upon Celtic traditions like the living Fairy Faith, where we form relationships of mutual respect and hospitality with those spirits who are willing.

For some ideas of how we deal with spirits who might be disruptive to us during ritual, see

✦ You talk a lot about the role of the Outsiders. What do you mean by that? (p. 91)

What is the difference between CR and Celtic Neopaganism?

"Celtic" Neopaganism, which is usually eclectic Neopaganism with some Celtic elements taken out of context, relies primarily on the ritual and philosophical models of the larger Neopagan community. It includes casting circles, the use of the athame and other tools from Ceremonial Magic, a model of four elements and four directions, and often embraces the Wiccan Rede as an ethical construct. Within this model, Neopagans may call upon Celtic Deities, though those Deities are usually seen through the lens of eclectic Neopaganism – triple Goddesses who are sisters in the original Celtic lore are frequently re-interpreted as Maiden-Mother-Crone triads. Gods are re-interpreted as solar and Goddesses as lunar, when this pattern is not actually a part of early Celtic belief. Antlered Gods are envisioned as Hunting Gods instead of Mercurial transfunctional Deities associated with crossing boundaries. The modern eightfold wheel of the year is used rather than focusing on actual Celtic cultural and seasonal festivals.

"Celtic" Neopaganism relies more on magic and spellcasting than CR tends to. Where "Celtic" Neopaganism often employs language suggesting the Gods and Goddesses can be "used" or commanded, and images of invocation and dismissal, CR focuses on developing mutual tribal or familial relationships through practices of offering, hospitality and invitation. CR is more likely to conceptualize dealing with Deities as a process of prayer, appeal, and mutual affection rather than invocation and spellwork. "Celtic" Neopaganism often rejects the label of religion in favor of spirituality, while CR embraces both religion and spirituality as valid ways of approaching human relationship with the sacred.

CR Paganism does not embrace Wiccan or eclectic Neopagan models for ritual or ethics, but looks instead to older, Celtic models. Our cosmology is different, our ethics come from a very different worldview, and our approach to the Divine is different as well. CR, in many ways, bears more resemblance to animistic tribal religions than to modern eclectic Neopaganism. In CR there is more emphasis on ancestors (wherever they may hail from) and local land spirits than in "Celtic" Neopaganism. Warrior paths are embraced rather than rejected. Sacrifice in certain contexts is accepted as a part of the religion where "Celtic" Neopaganism generally shies from the idea.

In "Celtic" Neopaganism, ritual tends to be seen as separate from daily life, performed at the seasonal days and on full or new moons. CR Paganism embraces the small, everyday acts of purification, devotion and focus as a part of an everflowing pattern of ritual that moves from rising in the morning to going to sleep at night.

Some CRs feel that Eclectic Neopaganism which incorporates Celtic elements is an acceptable part of the Celtic continuum, and that this diversity should be encouraged. Other CRs feel that eclectic, "Celtic" Neopaganism should never be called Celtic as it is only taking bits of Celtic culture out of context, and in this process sometimes obscuring actual Celtic beliefs and practices. Many believe that, even if unintentional, this misrepresentation of eclectic practices and beliefs as Celtic is a form of cultural imperialism.

See also

✧ Why do CRs hate Wicca and Wiccans? (p. 77)
✧ Who can initiate me into your super-duper secret tradition handed down from the early mists of time? You are the "hidden children of the Goddess," right? (p. 70)
✧ Are you Gaelic Traditionalists? What is the difference between Traditionalism and Reconstructionism? (p. 134)

Is Celtic Christianity a part of CR?

Celtic Reconstructionists are dedicated to reviving ancient Celtic religion. The ancient Celts were polytheists.

That said, with its veneration of many divine beings (saints), and its reverence for nature and contemplation, early Celtic Christianity was not that different from the Paganism which preceded it. Whereas the Great-Grandmother of an early Celtic Christian may have prayed to Bríde, Manannán and Lugh, in praying to Saints Brigid and Michael, the Celtic Christians maintained a significant amount of the imagery and rituals sacred to many of the *Déithe*. Similarly, a modern CR may take the rituals and prayers their Great-Grandmother made to the Celtic saints and, through research in the manuscripts that preserved the older tales, "back-engineer" these nominally Christian practices to what may have been their original, Pagan state.

Through this work, we are somewhat familiar with Celtic Christianity. Those of us who participate in the living Celtic cultures also interact with Christians regularly, as most people in the living Celtic cultures are Christian. Though Christianity as a religion is not part of CR, CRs and Celtic Christians value many of the same holy days and places of pilgrimage. It is not at all uncommon to find ourselves kneeling next to Christians at the same holy well. Though the particular prayers we say are somewhat different, as is the theology behind them, we are still able to see ourselves as travelers on related paths. Christianity may not be our religion, but we are able to find common ground and peace with many Christians.

Those of us who participate in the living Celtic cultures, or who belong to large, extended families, have often experienced events that combine Pagan and Christian elements. An Irish wake, for example, may have a section where a Catholic will say the rosary, then an agnostic will make a toast, then the Pagan will tell a story of the ancestors who have gone before and now welcome the deceased to the Otherworld. The Pagan may also make sure that some of the food is set aside in offering to the departed, and that some of the "toast" is spilled out in libation to the spirits. Obviously, these things work best when everyone involved is tolerant of a variety of religious approaches. But, in our experience, as long as these practices are situated firmly within the cultural context, it is rare for there to be any conflict between the approaches.

See also
✧ Is this a religion, or a culture? (p. 22)

Do you practice Celtic shamanism?

Short answer: No.

Longer answer: Many of us find the use of the term "shamanism" problematic, as it is a term which refers to a specific spiritual/religious complex in a specific, non-Celtic, culture (Tungus/Siberian). The word "shamanism" came into common usage as anthropologists noted some similarities between the practices of a few differing and unrelated traditional peoples. They began using the term, loosely, to refer to these varying practices. However it has always been a rather superficial generalization that did not accurately fit many of the cultures described. That usage has traveled, and become even broader and less useful, into the Neopagan and occultist lexicons (largely due to the controversial work of Michael Harner).

To call any mystical practices which deal with the spirit worlds "shamanism" is unfair to the culture which originated the term, and to those other cultures which are subsequently lumped together and homogenized. It fosters a sort of spiritual laziness, where culture-specific practices are mistaken for universal, and which often prevents seekers from looking deeper to the actual practices of the culture in question.

While there are certainly mystical aspects to some parts of CR practice, and a strong tradition of work with spirits and the spirit worlds, CR practitioners generally feel that "shamanism" is an inappropriate and potentially offensive word to describe what we do. We have perfectly serviceable words for what we do in the Celtic languages – words which actually describe our historical practices – and we prefer to refer to ourselves by those titles if and when we earn them. Some of these titles are *draoí, file, awenydd*, and others.

Who do I pay to be initiated into Celtic Shamanism?

Nobody. We aren't Celtic Shamans, nor do we actually believe there were Celtic "shamans" per se, so we can't offer you any initiations like that.

Are you Gaelic Traditionalists? What is the difference between Traditionalism and Reconstructionism?

If a tradition has to be pieced together from fragmentary survivals, books and folklore, it is Reconstructionism. If there is a community of people already following an intact tradition, complete with a full system of belief and practices they can teach you, that means you are joining an existing tradition.

In the early years of the CR movement, we probably tended to gravitate towards calling ourselves reconstructionists, not traditionalists, because of our commitment to accuracy and honesty, and our respect for the living cultures. While there are ancient manuscripts and books of 19th century folklore that describe things similar to what we wanted, there was no living tradition that had preserved a complete, polytheistic Celtic religion as part of the living culture. There were Catholics with some easily re-Paganized bits. There were the piles of obscure books. There were some small survivals of practices, beliefs and attitudes in some of our families of origin, but no complete spiritual system. There was no polytheistic, traditional Celtic community to join. So, we began the process of putting the pieces back together – reconstructing.

At that point, it never would have occurred to us to call ourselves any sort of Celtic or Gaelic "Traditionalists." Those words already had meanings in the living cultures, especially in the Gaelic areas of Ireland and Scotland. Had it even occurred to us to do so, adopting that name would have felt arrogant or, at the least, inappropriate – especially as the approach we were taking to this was somewhat new.

The Neopagan communities have a problematic history of fabricated traditions being passed off as survivals of ancient religions. So, even as we began speaking about how our developing traditions relied on the older sources, we needed to make sure people understood that we were not pretending to be the secret keepers of vast, ancient, occult, Celtique mysteries that we'd learned at the feet of our fictionalized Grandmothers or Grand Da's. (See also **Who can initiate me into your super-duper secret tradition handed down from the early mists of time? You are the "hidden children of the Goddess," right?** (p. 70))

So out of this need for rigorous honesty, at times we overstated the point. For instance, in *"The CR Essay,"*[19] we said things like, "CR makes no claims to being a True and Authentic Survival of any Celtic tradition. We acknowledge fully and openly that what we practice are a set of modern creations, based in and inspired by early Celtic beliefs." We probably would have been better off to phrase that as, "CR makes no claims to being a True and Authentic, Intact Survival of any complete pre-Christian Celtic Pagan tradition." We did not for a moment mean anything like "we make stuff up and call it Celtic," though, apparently, some misread it to mean exactly that. We meant that the way we are doing this, though based upon the ways of the ancestors and the surviving fragments in our communities, is not coming from a complete, unbroken line. It is old, in that we look to old sources and have some small pieces of intact survivals, but it is also new. As we live in modern times, it will not be identical to what our ancestors did. And as almost all the people in the living Celtic cultures are Christians, what we are doing will not be identical to their approach, either.

While the broader umbrella of CR includes people of all the Celtic cultures, it does seem that most CRs are reconstructing Gaelic forms of polytheism, or interested in participating in groups that have laid down some foundations in these areas. Those of us doing this also participate in the broader, traditional Gaelic cultures via language study/preservation, and participation in Gaelic traditional art forms and other cultural activities.

There are now also groups of polytheists who call themselves Gaelic Traditionalists (GT). In order to distinguish them from the Traditional Gaels in the *Gaeltacht/Gàidhealtachd* areas of Ireland and Scotland, or the traditional Gaelic cultural activities mentioned elsewhere in this FAQ, some Irish and Scottish observers of the phenomenon have suggested these GTs be called Modern American Gaelic Traditionalists (MAGT) – as the modern, polytheistic tradition began in America, from similar origins as

---

[19] *www.witchvox.com/trads/trad_cr.html*

CR, and at around the same time as the CR movement was beginning to take shape. Another proposed name change, by some of the elders of the American movement, is "Diasporic Gaelic Traditionalists" (DGT). Using either of these names instead of "GT" helps avoid confusion with the older, Irish and Scottish groups, as well as some of the tension and misunderstandings that have arisen from the name "Gaelic Traditionalists."

Many of those who identify as GT or DGT have practices and beliefs that are indistinguishable from CR, and the differing name is just a matter of personal preference. However, despite the common origins of our movements, our increasing visibility on the Internet has in more recent years attracted individuals who want to use our names but do not share our values or ethics. There are some who have recently called themselves GT but have created something that in no way resembles the values, beliefs, nor practices of CR, nor even those of early GT or DGT.

Right now, DGT is largely a different community from CR, with a different tone and flavor. However there is, and has always been, some overlap between the communities, as well as cooperation and mutual respect between some of the founders of both movements. There have also been some quite serious disagreements between the elders of CR and some of the newer MAGTs, usually over issues of ethical violations and dishonesty among some of the newcomers. However, those seem to have mostly involved fringe elements of MAGT, people who have at various times called themselves "druids," "CR," or "GT" while in actuality sharing none of the core values of any of our communities. Thankfully, it appears those disruptive elements have now moved on to experimenting with yet another identity, and the core members of the CR and GT communities will continue to build solidarity and set limits on those whose beliefs and behaviours are unacceptable in our communities.

Just as we have no real control over who chooses to self-identify as CR, or over the behaviour of those who call themselves CR, neither can the GTs or DGTs completely control the use of their names. What we can do is state clearly what our principles are, what is and isn't acceptable behaviour in our communities, and take a stand when someone steps outside the bounds of acceptable behaviour.

Chapter Ten

So you want to be CR...

What can I do to get started?

Getting started is fairly easy and there are many things you can do even if you don't have access to a large CR community or a research library.

Reading is very important in getting started in CR. Knowing the history of the Celtic peoples helps connect us with those times and places, and gives us the background to understand what the Gods and Goddesses are telling us. Start with the introductory books listed here: **Which books for someone totally new to CR?** (p. 145) These are easily available and not overwhelming. Start working your way through the reading lists at your own pace, taking time to absorb and integrate the ideas as you begin to formulate ways to put them into practice in your own life.

Find some space in your home or outdoors near where you live and create an altar or a shrine for the Deities, for your ancestors, or for the land spirits. Make offerings to them there – water and small bits of food on a plate will do, though more elaborate offerings will be welcome. Milk products, baked goods, apples, rowan berries, oats and hazelnuts are all traditional, but many people simply offer some of the best of their own meals.

Contemplate the world as a cosmology of land, sea and sky, everpresent around you. Feel how you are connected to the three realms. Meditate on the well and tree that are at the center of the worlds and which link all things together; and upon the gateways to the Otherworlds that can open in the center or at the edges.

Meditate on the fire that arises from the well – signaling the presence of the Deities, and the awakening of *iomas* (inspiration).

If you are not already, become involved in the living Celtic cultures. Seek out language classes, traditional storytelling and music *seisiúns* or *cèilidhs*, performances or classes in traditional dance and martial arts forms, and Highland Games or other Celtic festivals. Become acquainted with the surviving traditions in the Celtic nations and the diaspora, and meditate on the ways in which the largely-Christian practices are the same or different from a polytheistic approach. Listen to music and radio in the languages of the Celtic cultures you are drawn to. Become familiar with how language shapes thought, and how the mindset of a culture is revealed in the structure of the language.

Community is a core value of CR. Put some time and energy into forming connections with others on the path, in person if you can, and online if that is all that is available to you. Even for those of us who are lucky to have in-person CR communities, the online world is very important as it gives us access to a worldwide community of pooled research and experience. (See **Are there any CR organizations? Websites? Books?** (p. 37))

Take time every day to meditate on the Celtic Deities Who call you, and listen to Their voices. Read the tales about Them and think about what those tales mean. Find ways to bring Their presence into your life through use of images, music, or colors that you associate with Them. Find places in nature that seem special to Them, such as the seashore or a forest, a field or mountain or well, or even a small pond or special tree in a city park. Spend time there in meditation and making offerings. Be alert to the signs of the Deities' presence in your life.

On your indoor shrines, in addition to food and drink, burn candles and herbs or incense for the Deities and spirits as offerings.

Pay attention to your dreams and write them down. The Deities and spirits often communicate with us through the agency of dreams. Check with others who are CR in online communities or in your area if your dreams and impressions raise questions for you.

Juniper was traditionally used as an herb of purification in Scotland and many Scottish and Irish based CRs burn it to purify themselves and their space. You can do this by burning small amounts of juniper and letting it smolder in any fireproof container. Many CRs do this before making offerings, at the beginning of rituals, or as part of their meditations.

Celebrate the festivals with a feast and make offerings to the Deities, ancestors and spirits when you do so. Even if your friends and family aren't CR themselves, everyone loves to get together for a shared meal. Even the staunchest of Christians also appreciate tales of the ancestors, heroes and heroines of history, so traditional music and storytelling can easily be incorporated into religious or non-religious festivals.

Get outside and connect with the spirits of the land. Make offerings to them and talk to them. Most importantly, listen to them.

Breathe. Love. Laugh.

Live.

See also

✦ Offerings seem to be a really important part of all those rituals. How do I make offerings? (p. 107)

I have kids. How can I include them in all this?

While it may seem most public CRs are childless, this is perhaps because those without children simply have more time to be discussing it. CR is actually very child friendly due to having both cultural and religious aspects, celebratory rituals rather than only "working" rituals, and being open to many ways of approaching the paths. This allows parents to include their children at whatever level their interest and attention span determines. Children tend to learn well by inclusion, so rather than "teaching" them the religion, most CR parents simply include them in activities and discuss the purposes of those activities as they go, and go into detail only when the children ask.

As storytelling is a major part of Celtic cultures as well as a favored activity for many parents and children, this is often a starting point for CR parents. Some parents might feel more comfortable just reading the stories to and with their children, but others might spend time memorizing the stories in order to retell them from memory as a way to both share with their children and become more familiar themselves with the tales.

Older children who are interested may want to learn storytelling themselves.

CR parents usually include their children in making routine offerings. The entire family might gather at the household shrine, yard or outdoor location to give to the Deities, ancestors and spirits. In some families it's actually the job of the children to make the offerings or they may make specific ones while other family members do others. The children may want to help decorate the shrines and/or may have one in their own rooms. These may be kept very general, or as the child shows interest in a particular Deity, spirit or ancestor (usually for children this interest would be in a loved one who they remember who has passed) objects relating to those Beings might be included.

Many groups which include families allow young children to come and go from a ritual area as long as a parent or guardian is keeping an eye on them to keep them from wandering off or into the fire. Many times the children are kept in mind in designing the rituals, which may also help keep the rituals more interesting for less mystically minded adults. This includes giving the children roles such as helping with offerings, helping to pass out food or drink that might be shared in ritual, or short phrases to say. Ritual drama and storytelling regarding the season being celebrated also help children, as well as adults, feel connected to the ceremony's purpose. The one exception for including children in seasonal celebrations is *Oíche Shamhna*, which is considered by some CRs to be a dangerous time, especially for children. Also, groups that do ritual drama often do things at *Oíche Shamhna* that might be too intense for young children. This may lead to a children's party/ritual being done indoors with some of the parents, allowing them to still participate in the festival, while allowing most of the adults to have their intensity, with everyone getting together for a feast afterwards.

Children's culture can reveal many small survivals of traditional lore. Some of the old traditions have been preserved as children's games, rhymes and dances. Customs often ignored by adults, or dismissed as superstitions, have sometimes been maintained by the children and passed down by older children to younger ones in an informal, cultural way, for many generations. What may have once been a solemn ritual becomes a children's party. A tribal Deity or ancestor may now be a ghost story told at girls' slumber parties. Divination "games," in particular, have preserved some old ways of interaction with the spirits, and bonfire parties at *Oíche Shamhna* and *Lá Bealtaine* were a part of some of our childhoods. With the advent of television, much of this children's culture has now been damaged, and is in need of preservation. But some older members of the CR community who grew up in Celtic neighborhoods experienced these things as an integral part of our childhoods.

As children tend to learn languages more easily than adults, some CR parents expose their children to the language of their culture. For those who themselves are not fluent, this may include language and song tapes very early on, and the possibility of classes if the older children are interested.

Just as many adult CRs find Celtic cultural societies offer a great deal to enrich their connection to the culture, often these organizations also offer play groups, classes and other activities for children. Highland, Step and other dance classes for children are much easier to find than for adults and offer a fun connection to the culture that may have great meaning for the child as they grow. Cultural events such as Highland Games and Irish Festivals, which feature animals, music and other entertainment, often have a great deal of attraction for children as well.

See also
✧ Which books for kids? (p. 151)

I'm told that I should practice hospitality. What does that mean?

Hospitality is one of the premier virtues among the Celtic peoples, both ancient and modern. Its practice can be as simple as making sure any guest you have is offered a warm welcome, cup of tea and a snack, or as elaborate as making sure you always have room for unexpected overnight guests who might need a place to stay. The art of hospitality may include creative cooking to stretch things a little for company. It might just mean being a sympathetic ear to a friend who needs one.

Most CR folk, even those of us who tend to be social hermits, are often fond of visitors and conversation over a hot drink on a cold winter evening. Many of the Irish triads address issues of hospitality. Here are a few:

Trí fuiric thige degduni: cuirm, fothrucud, tene mór.
> Three preparations of a good man's house: ale, a bath, a large fire.

Trí fuiric thige drochduni: debuid ar do chinn, athchosan frit, a chú dot gabáil.
> Three preparations of a bad man's house: strife before you, complaining to you, his hound taking hold of you.

Trí fiada co n-anfhiad: gréss i nóentig fri muintir, uisce rothé dar cosa, bíad goirt cen dig.
> The three worst welcomes: a handicraft in the same house with the inmates, scalding water upon the feet, salt food without a drink.

Trí fáilti coirmthige: immed 7 dúthracht 7 elathó.
> Three welcomes of an alehouse: plenty and kindliness and art.

Hospitality works both ways, though. There are expectations of the guest as well as of the host. Traditionally it was said "a tale from the host, then tales from the guest until sunrise." This reflects a time when news was hard to come by, and any traveler would bring information from afar. Stories and songs were shared, as well as gossip and important news about the world outside the croft.

While it might be reasonable to expect, as a guest, to be invited in if you show up unannounced (unless the hosts are on their way out the door), good guest behavior would dictate letting someone know you're showing up. Bringing a gift of some sort is generally part of good hospitality if you're visiting someone you rarely see. Being polite under another's roof, treating their children, housemates, and animals well, and expressing gratitude for hospitality are also valued. As a guest, it's expected that you don't fight with your host, steal from them, or leave their home in worse shape than it was when you came to visit.

Online, we also have expectations of hospitality on our email lists and in our electronic communities. Some of these expectations are that you will be polite to each other and the hosts, that you'll do some looking into areas of interest offline before asking questions, and that you'll follow up your assertions with documentation if it's requested. Where lists and communities have rules, those rules should be read and followed whenever possible. Requests are always going to be treated more favorably than demands of your hosts and the regulars on the lists.

If I'm going to be CR, how should I wear my hair?

The Path of the Hairdo® is a very important part of Celtic Reconstructionism. You may spike up your hair with Bog Body Hair Gel® (sold on our official website). Alternately, you may wear The Official CR Tonsure™, which involves shaving bits of hair off your head when you are bored or in a deep trance of devotion to your Gods. It is also traditional to cut or shave the hair when in mourning, and this must be done with appropriate wailing, bellowing, and gnashing of teeth.

There is a schism who both tonsure and spike, with lime or Bog Gel®, but that is an inner mystery, not suitable for a public forum. Others firmly believe that no hairdo is an official CR hairdo unless it involves braiding it and then running through the woods while people throw spears at you. Then being buried in the ground up to your waist and fending off more spear attacks. This camp is adamant that, if your hair gets messed up during this challenge, it is not worthy of being considered a Real CR Hairdo®.

Those who have adopted The Official CR Tonsure™ must also tattoo, or daily paint, symbols of their path on the revealed canvas. There is a great deal of controversy in these matters, as those who have chosen to tattoo believe everyone else with The Official CR Tonsure™ must endure the same pain they did. Those who are allergic to tattoo inks must simply find other ways to cause themselves pain. Such as answering endless bizarre questions in online fora when sensible people would be sleeping. Or that's what I've heard. What?

Seriously? Wear your hair any way you want. We're kidding. Mostly.

Chapter Eleven

The Ever-Popular Reading List Section

Which books for someone totally new to CR?

Gods and Heroes of the Celts – Marie-Louise Sjoestedt
This is an excellent introduction to Celtic mythology in a variety of cultures. It's short and clear, emphasizing the importance of not attempting to smoosh Celtic Deities into Classical Mediterranean models. A wonderful overview.

Celtic Mythology – Proinsias Mac Cana
This coffee-table style book is a wonderful introduction to Celtic myth as well, and includes fabulous color photos of artifacts and archaeological sites. It's an easy read and covers a great deal of territory.

Celtic Heritage – Alwyn and Brinley Rees
A more complex read than the others, Celtic Heritage relies very heavily on Dumézilian models and comparisons to Hindu religion. While these comparisons are useful, many in Dumézil's camp tend to rely too heavily on Hindu models and view Celtic religion as almost identical in structure, if not in practice. It is important to remember that Celtic and Hindu cultures are in fact different, and that while similarities can help illuminate gaps in the Celtic records, it is not wise to attempt to import ritual and pattern in toto from one culture to another.

A Circle of Stones – Erynn Rowan Laurie
A book of practical exercises written by a CR elder for the CR community. The author states that she would present the

material differently now, given her many more years of research and experience, but the practices presented and the materials on altars are extremely useful for those on an Irish or Scottish CR path.

Which three books are most important?

Four General Celtic Books:

Myths and Symbols in Pagan Europe – H.R. Ellis Davidson
Celtic Mythology – Proinsias Mac Cana
Celtic Heritage – Alwyn & Brinley Rees
Gods and Heroes of the Celts – Marie-Louise Sjoestedt (translated by Myles Dillon from the original French *Dieux et Héros des Celtes*)

Three Scottish Books:

The Gaelic Otherworld – John Gregorson Campbell, ed. by Ronald Black
Carmina Gadelica – Alexander Carmichael
The Silver Bough – F. Marian MacNeil

Three Irish Books:

The Year in Ireland – Kevin Danaher
Irish Folk Ways – E. Estyn Evans
The Wisdom of the Outlaw – Joseph Falaky Nagy

Three Welsh Books:

Trioedd Ynys Prydein: The Triads of the Island of Britain – Rachel Bromwich
The Mabinogi and Other Welsh Medieval Tales – Patrick K. Ford
Ystoria Taliesin – Patrick K. Ford

Two Gaulish Books:

The Celtic Gauls: Gods, Rites and Sanctuaries – Jean-Louis Brunaux
Lady With A Mead Cup – Michael Enright

Which books do you recommend?

Celtic Art – George Bain
A Military History of Ireland – Thomas Bartlett and Keith Jeffery, eds.
Healing Threads – Mary Beith
Irish Bardic Poetry – Osborn Bergin
Auraicept na n-Éces: The Scholars Primer – George Calder, ed.

The Gaelic Otherworld – John Gregorson Campbell, ed. Ronald Black
Carmina Gadelica – Alexander Carmichael
Medieval Irish Lyrics with The Irish Bardic Poet – James Carney
The Great Queens – Rosalind Clark
A Guide to Britain's Pagan Heritage – David Clarke
Twilight of the Celtic Gods – David Clarke and Andy Roberts
Fairy Legends and Traditions of the South of Ireland – Thomas Crofton
 Croker
Ancient Irish Tales – Cross and Slover
The Ancient Celts – Barry Cunliffe
The Celtic World – Barry Cunliffe
Mythic Ireland – Michael Dames
The Year in Ireland – Kevin Danaher
Myths and Symbols in Pagan Europe – H. R. Ellis Davidson
Early Irish Literature – Myles Dillon
Tales of the Elders of Ireland – tr. by Ann Dooley and Harry Roe
Lady With a Mead Cup – Michael Enright
Irish Folk Ways – E. Estyn Evans
The Mabinogion - tr. by Patrick K. Ford
The Tory Islanders – Robin Fox
The Philosopher and the Druids: A Journey Among the Ancient Celts –
 Philip Freeman
Early Irish Myths and Sagas – tr. by Jeffrey Gantz
The History of the Kings of Britain – Geoffrey of Monmouth (tr. by
 Lewis Thorpe)
Irish Folktales – Henry Glassie
Passing the Time in Ballymenone – Henry Glassie
Celtic Goddesses – Miranda Green[20] (This is a qualified recommendation)
Dictionary of Celtic Myth and Legend – Miranda J. Green (This is a
 qualified recommendation)
Gods of the Celts – Miranda Green (This is a qualified recommendation)
Symbol and Image in Celtic Religious Art – Miranda Green (This is a
 qualified recommendation)

---

[20] *Celtic Goddesses, Dictionary of Celtic Myth and Legend, Gods of the Celts, Symbol and Image in Celtic Religious Art, The World of the Druids* - While many consider these books to be accessible introductions to matters Celtic, and we do generally recommend them, there are some definite drawbacks to bear in mind. The author is an archaeologist who, at the time these books were written, had little or no facility with the Celtic languages. So while the archeology is generally sound, the lack of any Celtic language can create problems, especially in the author's interpretation of the old myths and tales. These books generally promote the "Solar God" hypothesis, which is an outmoded and non-Celtic conclusion. Similarly, the Deities are generally seen through a non-native, Classical view, which other authors (such as Sjoestedt) stress is an inaccurate way to approach the Celtic mythologies.

The World of the Druids – Miranda Green (This is a qualified recommendation)
A Golden Treasury of Irish Poetry – David Greene and Frank O'Connor
The Making of a Druid – Christian-J. Guyonvarc'h
Symbols of the Celts – Sabine Heinz
Survivals in Belief Among the Celts – George Henderson
A Celtic Miscellany – Kenneth Hurlstone Jackson
The World of the Celts – Simon James[21] (This is a qualified recommendation)
The Law of Hywel Dda – tr. by Dafydd Jenkins
The Mabinogion – tr. by Gwyn Jones and Thomas Jones
A Guide to Early Irish Law – Fergus Kelly
The Tain – tr. by Thomas Kinsella
The Celtic Heroic Age – John T. Koch and John Carey, eds.
The Apple Branch – Alexei Kondratiev[22] (This is a qualified recommendation)
A Circle of Stones – Erynn Rowan Laurie

---

[21] While generally useful as an introduction to the various Celtic cultures in antiquity, the author, Simon James, subscribes to a point of view known as "celtoskepticism." This is the idea that discussing "Celts," as such, is fruitless due to a supposed lack of continuity between the various peoples collectively known by that term. The view has its origin among some archaeologists and arises from a lack of perfect continuity of style between the artifacts left by various ancient Celtic peoples. The celtoskeptics also point to genetic studies which show no genetic basis for thinking of the groups as unified. From these, the celtoskeptics make the leap to dismissal of any continuity of culture, mythology, and religious practice. However, this celtoskeptic position is not generally held among folklorists, linguists, Indo-Europeanists, or most others who study Celtic cultures, all of whom note a distinct continuity of ideas among the various Celtic peoples (and, indeed, to a lesser extent a certain continuity with other Indo-European cultures, especially the Germano-Scandinavian ones).

The celtoskeptic view would be of no particular consequence to most living Celtic communities except that it has been used by some (though James has not, himself, used the stance in this manner) to undermine the efforts of members of Celtic cultural communities to take control of their own affairs.

It is ironic, of course, that a celtoskeptic would write a book which purports to discuss "Celts" as a single class. James does not explain his reasoning in the book, and for the most part the book seems to avoid at least the excesses of the celtoskeptic stance. However, because of the very real political danger that the stance holds to living Celtic cultural groups, we feel that some caution should be given in regard to this book, as well as the author's other writings on matters Celtic.

[22] Although some people like this book a great deal, and it is sometimes treated by some as though it were a definitive book on CR Pagan practices, most CRs note that it was composed before the CR community existed, and at a time when a more purely CR work had no appreciable market. (Though published in the late 1990s, the book was actually written in the mid-1980s.) As a result, many elements of the book make use of more general Neopagan ideas, and other elements which are not a part of CR belief or practice. In addition, the purpose of the book was not to present a CR method of practice, or to be about CR at all, but rather to present a form of culturally-based religion which was practical for groups including Neopagans, Wiccans, Christians, and others. The author himself has stated that it is not a CR book.

Furthermore, some interpretations of Celtic theology in the book are questioned by CRs, as is the ritual structure popularized in the book (and it is the latter which is the more important criticism.) While it is often included on some broad-based, CR-related reading lists, most CRs do not consider it a CR book. A significant number of CRs actually consider the book to be more misleading than helpful to those looking for information on CR.

Death, War, and Sacrifice – Bruce Lincoln
The Banshee: The Irish Death Messenger – Patricia Lysaght
Celtic Mythology – Proinsias Mac Cana
The Learned Tales of Medieval Ireland – Proinsias Mac Cana
The Religion of the Ancient Celts – J. A. MacCulloch
The Oxford Dictionary of Celtic Mythology – James MacKillop
In Search of the Indo-Europeans – J. P. Mallory
A Guide to Ogam – Damian McManus
The Silver Bough – F. Marian McNeill
Celtic Art – Ruth and Vincent Megaw
Ancient Irish Poetry – Kuno Meyer
A Primer of Irish Metrics – Kuno Meyer
Conversing With Angels and Ancients – Joseph Falaky Nagy
The Wisdom of the Outlaw – Joseph Falaky Nagy
A Handbook of the Scottish Gaelic World – Michael Newton.[23] (This is a
    qualified recommendation)
The Book of the Cailleach – Gearóid Ó Crualaoich
Celtic Consciousness – Robert O'Driscoll, ed.

---

[23] The authors of this FAQ believe Michael Newton's *Handbook of the Scottish Gaelic World* can be useful to CRs, especially for its emphasis on the importance of poetry and language in Gaelic culture. We also believe the book offers a degree of insight into the culture that is lacking in some other books. However, some of us, even though we otherwise recommend the book, have problems with some areas of the text. We are concerned these areas could be interpreted as sounding misogynist or racist, and could further be interpreted as saying that Gaelic culture is inherently misogynist and/or racist.

Those of us with these concerns feel that some readers may get the impression that Newton focuses on some of the most misogynist bits of lore he can find in the cultures, or worse, that such misogyny is totally reflective of the cultures. In some places he balances these sections with other less offensive examples, or examples that even cast women in a neutral or positive light. However, in a number of cases his writing could be interpreted as if he's actively promoting a woman-hating view. The concern is that the reader may decide misogyny is seen as acceptable in Gaelic culture and in the CR community. They may also mistakenly believe that by recommending this book, we are somehow promoting those views.

Newton's writing can also be internally inconsistent. On one page, he'll lambaste the Victorian-era revivalists for their Noble Savage approach to the field of study (and all the attendant problems that causes), then elsewhere in the book he'll appear to take exactly the same romanticized approach himself. In one place he'll have a brief disclaimer about racism, then in other places he'll say some things that may appear to the reader to subtly promote the racist tendencies of "pride of the blood" which elsewhere he notes is an inaccurate concept.

We have absolutely no problem with authors accurately reporting the problematic parts of our ancestors' beliefs and behavior. It would be wrong to leave those things out, especially in cases where one is attempting a thorough overview. However, every author makes choices about which areas to focus on and whether to leave things uncommented-upon or to attempt to put them in some sort of context. The particular choices Newton made in a number of these areas make some of us uncomfortable with recommending this book without noting our concerns. We do generally recommend it, but parts it have made some of us uncomfortable and we are concerned others might draw the wrong conclusions about our community and beliefs were we not to express these concerns.

The Silva Gadelica – Standish O'Grady
Early Ireland – Michael J. O'Kelly
Welsh Folk Customs – Trefor Owen
Manx Calendar Customs – Cyril I. Paton
Cattle Lords & Clansmen – Nerys Patterson
Sex and Marriage in Ancient Ireland – Patrick C. Power
Pagan Celtic Ireland – Barry Raftery
Celtic Heritage – Alwyn and Brinley Rees
The Folklore of the Scottish Highlands – Anne Ross[24] (This is a qualified recommendation)
Pagan Celtic Britain – Anne Ross (This is a qualified recommendation)
The Pagan Celts – Anne Ross (This is a qualified recommendation)
Gods and Heroes of the Celts – Marie-Louise Sjoestedt (translated by Myles Dillon from the original French, *Dieux et Héros des Celtes*)
The Aran Islands – John M. Synge
The Secret Commonwealth and the Fairy Belief Complex – Brian Walsh
Beyond Celts, Germans, and Scythians – Peter S. Wells
The Fairy-Faith in Celtic Countries – W. Y. Evans Wentz[25] (This is a qualified recommendation)

Dictionaries

Y Geiriadur Newydd: The New Welsh Dictionary – Christopher Davies
English-Irish Dictionary – Tomás De Bhaldraithe
Foclóir Gaedhilge agus Béarla: Irish-English Dictionary – Patrick S. Dinneen
Geiriadur Prifysgol Cymru – Gareth Gareth, Gareth Bevan, and Patrick Donovan, eds. (Welsh)

---

[24] *Pagan Celtic Britain, The Pagan Celts, The Folklore of the Scottish Highlands* – Anne Ross is a respected Celtic scholar with a strong background in archaeology. There are some concerns, however, as Ross is another proponent of the outdated "Solar Gods" theories. This would not be of much concern, as most readers know to ignore the "Solar Gods" thing, except that she is often very determined in her attempts to offer proof, which can mar otherwise good information. However, *The Folklore of the Scottish Highlands* shows less tendencies towards this, perhaps because the material is primarily from the Christian period.

[25] While this is a tremendous piece of work, incorporating folklore, mythology, and more, it also suffers from the limitations of its time. Perhaps the most significant limitation is in its use of alien knowledge frameworks to "explain" the phenomena it records (such as its use of Theosophical speculations to give fairy-lore a "scientific" bent). Wentz is also, arguably, too credulous of his sources, sometimes accepting a single informant as authoritative. To be fair, no less a figure than Margaret Mead would later fall victim to the same error, but that doesn't save it from being potentially problematic (and, in fact, even Mead's work suffered from that mistake).

That said, as long as one bears those caveats in mind, this is considered by many to be an essential work, especially if one is working to develop a spiritual practice based on interactions with the spirit worlds. It provides a variety of accounts of the surviving practices of the ordinary Celtic peoples, and primary research not available in other books.

Dwelly's Gaelic Dictionary – Edward Dwelly (Scots Gaelic)
Foclóir Póca – An Gúm (Irish)
Etymological Dictionary of Scottish-Gaelic – Alexander MacBain
A Pronouncing and Etymological Dictionary of the Gaelic Language –
    Malcolm MacLennan (Scots Gaelic)
Foclóir Gaeilge-Béarla – Niall Ó Dónaill (Irish)
The Dictionary of the Irish Language – The Royal Irish Academy

Language Courses
Speaking Our Language – Cànan (Scots Gaelic)
Colloquial Welsh – Gareth King
Modern Welsh: A Comprehensive Grammar – Gareth King
Teach Yourself Gaelic – Roderick Mackinnon (Scots Gaelic)
Buntús Cainte – Tomas O Domhnallain (Irish)
Learning Irish – Mícheál Ó Siadhail
Grammar of Old Irish – R. Thurneysen (also includes some Gaulish
    and Welsh)

Which books for kids?

This is a short list of books that have received recommendations within various CR fora. This is neither meant to be a complete list nor is it necessarily meant to be a recommendation of these works by the compilers (though some of them are). Consider it rather to be a sampling of the diversity there is in the field of books for children that have Celtic themes to them.

Little Celtic Activity Book – Winky Adam
Finn MacCoul and His Fearless Wife: A Giant of a Tale From Ireland –
    Robert Byrd
The Silver Cow, a Welsh Tale – Susan Cooper
The Celts Activity Book – Mike Corbishly
The Wishing of Biddy Malone – Joy Cowley
Fin M'Coul: the Giant of Knockmany Hill – Tomie De Paola
Lucy Dove – Janice Del Negro
A Child's Book of Celtic Prayers – Joyce Denham (Illustrator), Helen
    Cann (Illustrator)
Celtic Gods and Heroes – John Green
Gods and Fighting Men – Lady Gregory
More Celtic Fairy Tales – Joseph Jacobs
The O'Brien Book of Irish Fairy Tales and Legends – Una Leavy

The Children of Lir – Sheila MacGill-Callahan
The Tain: The Great Celtic Epic – Liam MacUistin
Druids, Gods & Heroes from Celtic Mythology (World Mythology Series) – Anne Ross
Shape-Shifter, The Naming of Pangur Ban: Book One (The Pangur Ban Celtic Fantasies) – Fay Sampson
Pangur Ban the White Cat: Book Two (The Pangur Ban Celtic Fantasies) – Fay Sampson
Finnglas of the Horses: Book Three (The Pangur Ban Celtic Fantasies) – Fay Sampson
Life in Celtic Times – A. G. Smith
The Cool Maccool: Heroic Deeds of Finn Maccool Legendary Celtic Hero – Gordon Snell

There are so many translations, which ones do you recommend?

In order to make a reliable translation, the translator must be fluent in both the language they are translating from, and the language they are translating into. In addition, they must be an expert on the cultures from which those languages arise. As we have often stated in this FAQ, one cannot fully understand a culture without understanding the language of that culture. Similarly, one cannot make an accurate language translation without understanding the unique cultural contexts, beliefs of the culture's peoples, and idioms of those languages.

See also

✧ How do you pick which authors to believe? (p. 31)

Some Specific Recommendations

These are some editions which are known to be good translations of the source materials:

Tales of the Elders of Ireland – Ann Dooley and Harry Roe, trans.
The Mabinogi and Other Medieval Welsh Tales – Patrick K. Ford, trans.
The Second Battle of Maigh Tuiredh – Elizabeth Gray, trans.
The Mabinogion – Gwyn Jones and Thomas Jones, trans.
The Celtic Heroic Age – John T. Koch and John Carey, eds.

Which authors/publishers should I absolutely, without doubt, avoid like plague fleas?

This list is based on many people's experience and is specifically designed with CR in mind. For example, while Robert Graves has a poetic and evocative side to his writing, he is inaccurate and pretty much worthless in relation to Celtic subject matter. So while it may be difficult to make blanket statements and judgments, in relation to Celtic matters, we do feel qualified to steer you away from these authors and publishers.

Some inaccurate authors to stay away from:

- o   DJ Conway
- o   Murray Hope
- o   Kisma Stepanich
- o   Edain McCoy
- o   Tom Cowan
- o   Douglas Monroe
- o   Robert Graves
- o   Kaledon Naddair
- o   Francesca de Grandis
- o   Barry Fell
- o   Sirona Knight
- o   Iolo Morganwg
- o   Frank McEowen

Publishers who put out more questionable books than good ones:

- o   Llewellyn
- o   Capall Bann
- o   Elements

For reviews of several books both good and bad on Celtic Paganism and Druidism, with in-depth explanations of why they are considered good or bad books, we suggest the reviews on the *Digital Medievalist*[26] site.

Which authors/publishers are, with few exceptions, very reliable sources?

After careful consideration we have come to the (somewhat uncomfortable) conclusion that we can't provide you with a

---

[26] *http://www.digitalmedievalist.com/reviews/index.html*

definitive answer to this question. It is difficult to say an author will always be reliable, as people are fully capable of changing their minds, or spinning things differently for different publishers. Academic presses *tend* to be more reliable than occult presses as a general rule. Books on history and archaeology will most likely be more reliable than those on "Celtic Spirituality." We have pulled together a selection of reading lists that contain a number of books that are quite good on a variety of different topics relevant to CR.

See also
✦ Which books for someone totally new to CR? (p. 145)
✦ Which three books are most important? (p. 146)
✦ Which books for kids? (p. 151)
✦ There are so many translations, which ones do you recommend? (p. 152)
✦ Which books do you recommend? (the *long* list) (p. 146)

So how do I find this stuff?

In many areas, it can be hard to find good resources at your local bookshop. It's important to remember that most bookstores will do special orders for you if you ask. An excellent online bookshop for Celtic Studies books is **Books for Scholars**,[27] which carries many important and otherwise difficult to find texts, primarily in Welsh and Irish studies, but also for other Celtic cultures.

Used copies of the books you want can sometimes be found through **Abebooks**,[28] a site that acts as a central catalogue & order site for hundreds, if not thousands, of used bookstores around the world.

For books that are very expensive, you can check your local library, and if the books are not there, ask the librarian to help you with a process called Inter-Library Loan or ILL. This will bring a book you want from another library to your local library for you to borrow, and most US and Canadian libraries participate in these webs of information-sharing.

Another possibility, particularly for rare books or information that is difficult to find, are online editions. Many of the Irish-

---

[27] *http://www.booksforscholars.com/*
[28] *http://www.abebooks.com/*

language resources with translations are available at websites like the ***Irish Texts at CELT***[29] page or the translations of texts from many Celtic cultures at ***The Celtic Literature Collective***.[30] Searches for authors and particular out-of-copyright titles at ***Project Gutenberg***[31] can also be fruitful.

Sabhal Mòr Ostaig[32] maintains an online collection of Scots Gaelic texts, including the first volume of the ***Carmina Gadelica***,[33] an important source text for traditional prayers, spells and invocations from the Highlands and Islands, collected in the late 19th and early 20th centuries by Alexander Carmichael. Sabhal Mòr Ostaig is the premier Gaelic-language college in Scotland and has a wide variety of *Gàidhlig* language resources on its website. Volumes one and two of the Carmina can also be found at ***The Internet Sacred Texts Archive***.[34]

Resources exist, even for those with little or no money. It's just a matter of learning to look and knowing where to begin.

---

[29] *http://www.ucc.ie/celt/irlpage.html*
[30] *http://www.ancienttexts.org/library/celtic/ctexts/index.html*
[31] *http://www.gutenberg.org/*
[32] *http://www.smo.uhi.ac.uk/beurla/*
[33] *http://www.smo.uhi.ac.uk/gaidhlig/corpus/Carmina/*
[34] *http://www.sacred-texts.com/neu/celt/cg1/index.htm*

Pronunciation Guide

Pronunciation Key

All the living Celtic languages show remarkable dialect variation. You are likely to hear many of these words and names pronounced somewhat differently by people you meet, depending on which dialect(s) they speak or have learnt – and prepare also to hear them mangled by people who do not speak a Celtic language! What we have endeavored to do here is create a system of phonemic representation (adapted from the so-called "Gaelicist" system common in Irish scholarship) which will allow adequate representation of the sounds of several Celtic languages, and which indicates the underlying phonemes, the common base, from which the dialectal variation springs. This should allow you to pronounce things in a way which is intelligible to a speaker of the language regardless of which dialect(s) that person may speak. Of course, if you have access to a fluent or (if you are really lucky!) native speaker, then pronounce everything the way that he or she does! Old Irish (also known as Old Gaelic, since it is the ancestor language of all three modern Gaelics) is, of course, not spoken any more, so its pronunciation remains somewhat theoretical, like that of Latin or Classical Greek; we have done our best to give the most accurate, educated guesses possible, based largely upon how the living languages have changed or stayed the same over time.

Abbreviations: I = modern Irish. **OI** = Old Irish. **SG** = modern Scottish Gaelic. **W** = Welsh. **Sc** = Scots. **sing.** = singular. **pl.** = plural. **gen.** = genitive case.

Vowels

a as in *far*

e as in *met*

i as in *see*

o as in *port*

u as in *moon*

ɯ as **u** above, but pronounced with the lips spread wide and flat (for **u** the lips are rounded)

ə as in *about*

In the Celtic languages, vowels may be pronounced short or long. Long vowels are held twice as long in pronunciation as short vowels. There may be a difference in quality as well, but it is the length, not the quality of the vowel, which is the important distinguishing factor. Vowel length is especially important in the Gaelics, where it distinguished meanings of words: there are numerous pairs of words which are identical save for the length of the vowel. Long vowels are indicated by the symbol **:** following the vowel. For example, **a:** as in *barrage,* **e:** as in *strayed,* **i:** as in *agreed.*

Consonants

In the Gaelics, all consonants have two variants: unpalatalized or "hard," and palatalized or "soft." (The traditional names in Gaelic grammar for these, which you will probably encounter in textbooks and reference books, are "broad" and "slender" respectively.) Soft consonants are indicated in our transcription by a ′ symbol following the letter, for example, **d′**. Consonants not so marked, as in **d**, are hard. Perhaps the easiest way to approach most of the soft consonants is to try to pronounce a light "y" sound after them. "Back vowels" vs. "front vowels" are one of the determining factors in the pronunciation of consonants. The back vowels are a, o, u, and the front vowels are e, i.

b as in *but*

b′ before back vowels (a, o, u) like the "by" sound in *beauty;* otherwise as in *beak*

d as in *do*, but with the tongue pressed against the upper teeth, rather than on the ridge behind them as in English

d′ in northern Irish, Scottish Gaelic and Manx, a "j" sound as in *judge*; in other Irish dialects, varies from a "d" pronounced with the tongue tip on the alveolar ridge behind the upper teeth – in other words, like the English **d** – to a sound rather like "dz" as in *spades*

f as in *fool*

f′ before back vowels (a, o, u), like the "fy" sound in *few*; otherwise as in *fee*

g as in *go*

g′ a "gy" sound as in *argue*

h as in *home*

k as in *cool*

k′ a "ky" sound as in *cute*

l as in *leaf* – a light "l" sound made with just the tip of the tongue on the ridge behind the upper teeth

L as in *fall* – a thick "l" sound made by pressing the front of the tongue against the upper teeth

l′ an "ly" sound as in *million*

m as in *move*

m′ before back vowels (a, o, u), a "my" sound as in *meow*; otherwise as in *mean*

n as in *night* – a light "n" sound made with just the tip of the tongue on the ridge behind the upper teeth

N as in *found* – a thick "n" sound, made by pressing the front of the tongue against the upper teeth

n′ an "ny" sound as in *canyon*

p as in *pool*

p′ before back vowels (a, o, u), a "py" sound as in *pew*; otherwise as in *peel*

r in Scottish Gaelic and Welsh, a trill or tap of the tip of the tongue; this was the original pronunciation in Irish as well, and most likely the way it was pronounced in Old Irish; in modern Irish, the English "r" sound is common

r′ varies widely between dialects, from a single tap of the tip of the tongue, to an "r" sound with a "z" like quality to it, to practically a "z" sound; in Scottish Gaelic often a voiced "th" sound as in **this**

R a voiceless trilled "r" sound; try to pronounce a trilled "r" as in Spanish *perro*, in a whisper, without the vocal cords vibrating

s as in *so*

s′ an "sh" sound as in **shut**

t as in *to*, but with the tongue pressed against the upper teeth, rather than on the ridge behind them as in English

t′ in northern Irish, Scottish Gaelic and Manx, a "ch" sound as in *cheap*; in other Irish dialects, varies from a "t" pronounced with the tongue tip on the alveolar ridge behind the upper teeth – in other words, like the English **t** – to a sound rather like "ts" as in *cats*

v in Scottish Gaelic, Munster Irish, Standard Irish and Welsh, as in *vote*; in western and northern Irish, often a "w" sound as in **wet**, especially at the start of a word

v′ as in *veer*

w as in *wet*

y as in *yes*

x as in Scots *loch*, German *ach*, Russian *xo*; the linguistic description is a voiceless velar fricative

x′ as in German *ich*; somewhat similar to the "hy" sound in *huge*

ɣ as in Spanish *luego*, modern Greek *γάλα*; the linguistic description is a voiced velar fricative, that is, the voiced counterpart of **x**; English speakers tend to pronounce this sound too forcefully, as it is unfamiliar to modern English – it is actually a very soft, gentle sound

ɣ′ as in *yet*

θ voiceless "th" as in **think**

ð voiced "th" as in **that**

ð′ similar to ð followed by "y" as in *bathe you*; however, this sound doesn't exist in English, and no one knows for certain how it was pronounced; the linguistic description is a palatalized voiced dental fricative

ŋ as in *sing*

ɫ a voiceless, almost hissing sound produced by placing the tongue in the position for l above and then forcing the air out around the side of the tongue; the linguistic description is a voiceless lateral fricative; often wrongly described as a sort of "hl" or "thl" sound, which is not correct

Stress accent

In the Gaelics, the stress is usually on the first syllable of the word. In Welsh, the stress is usually on the penultimate (second to last) syllable. Stressed syllables deviating from these rules will be underlined.

Reconstructed Forms

Most Gaulish words are reconstructions. Reconstructed forms are indicated with an asterisk (*) preceding the word.

Glossary

Acallam na Senórach /aːɡəLəv nə sˈenoːrax/ (OI "colloquy of elders, ramblings of geezers") Important text of the Fenian Cycle of Irish literature, in which St. Patrick learns the place-name lore and adventures of Fionn and his *fianna* through having it related directly to him by Fionn's warriors, who have been brought forward in time in order to do so.

aicme /akˈmˈə/ (I "genus, class; tribe") A set of five *ogham* characters.

Áine /aːnˈə/ (I "brightness, glow, radiance; splendour, glory, fame") Local sovereignty Goddess associated with Cnoc Áine (Knockainy) in east Co. Limerick, in the south of Ireland. Sometimes symbolized by the bright sun of summer and the red mare. In later texts, seen as a "Fairy Queen" and associated with midsummer and love, though also known to bring vengeance when wronged.

Airmid /aːrˈəvˈiðˈ/ (OI) Goddess of herbalism and healing. Gathered together and memorized all the healing herbs of the world, which grew from Her murdered brother Miach's grave when watered by Her tears of mourning. When he saw what She had done, Her jealous father, Dian Cécht, scattered the herbs. This is said to be the reason no one except Airmid knows the properties of every herb.

aisling /asˈlənˈ/ (I/SG "dream") A mystical, Otherworldly vision. Some CRs use the term to refer to dreamwork or ritual that involves the seeking of visions.

Amairgen /aːvaːrˈgˈən/ (OI) Poet and judge of the Milesians who negotiated with the three Goddesses of the land of Ireland

(Fótla, Banba, and Ériu) to allow his people to land on the island. By reciting mystical poems identifying himself with all of creation and invoking the power and beauty of the land of Ireland, he succeeded in allowing the Milesians to land.

Anu /aːnu/ (OI, also Ana) Goddess of Ireland, considered by some to be synonymous with Áine and/or Danu, and by others to be a separate Goddess. Said to be the mother of the Gods in *Sanas Cormaic* and associated with the "Paps of Anu" near Killarney in Co. Kerry. Some CRs associate Her with the sky and the moon, others with the land.

Annwfn /anuːvən/ (W, also Annwn /anuːn/) Welsh word for the Otherworld, either reached via sea voyage or coexistent with the mundane world and yet invisible.

Aoife /iːfə/ (I) Scottish warrior woman and chieftain. Rival of the renowned martial arts teacher Scáthach, engaged in combat with Cú Chulainn.

Aos Sí /iːs sʹiː/ (I) The Irish Fairy Folk, the people of the mounds. Also, but less commonly, *Daoine Sí* /diːnʹə sʹiː/ (OI *Áes Síde* or *Áes Sídhe* /ais sʹiːðʹə/) See *Daoine-Sìth*.

Áes Sídhe /ais sʹiːðʹə/ (OI) See *Aos Sí, Daoine-Sìth*.

Arianrhod /arianRod/ (W) Welsh Goddess from the *Mabinogi*, mother of Llew Llaw Gyffes and sister of Gwydion, associated with the Corona Borealis.

Arawn /araun/ (W) Welsh God, aka *Pen Annwfn* ("Head/Chief of the Otherworld"), who in the *Mabinogi* makes an alliance with the king of Dyfed and trades commodities such as pigs with him in return for his help in a supernatural combat.

Ásatrú /aːsatruː/ (Icelandic/Old Norse) Reconstructed Norse polytheism. Also includes Germanic and Anglo-Saxon traditions.

Auraicept na nÉces /aurəkʹept nə neːgʹəs/ (OI "Primer of Scholars/Poets") Text detailing the origins of the Irish language and poetic laws, including the Ogham Tract detailing the *crannogham* (tree *ogham*, aka *crann ogham*) and other forms of the *ogham* alphabet.

awenydd /awenið/ (W "visionary poet," pl. *awenyddion* /awenəðyon/) Descriptions in Gerald of Wales suggest the *awenyddion* may have been in a type of possession trance during their divinatory work, as they are said to have lost complete control of their words and bodies.

Balor /baloːr/ (OI) King of the Fomorians, aka "Balor of the Evil or Baleful Eye." Cast in a negative light in many sources, but regarded by the Tory Islanders as a benign, grandfatherly Deity who was ousted by His grandson Lugh, who was seen as a young upstart.

Banba /baːnəbə/ (OI) Ancient Goddess of Ireland who, along with Ériu and Fótla, gave Her name to the entire island in return for helping Amairgen and the Milesians in their victory over the Túatha Dé Danann.

bàrd /baːrd/ (SG "poet") See *file*, *filidecht*.

bata /batə/ (I/SG "stick; baton") A club or walking stick, usually made from oak or blackthorn. Used in some forms of Celtic martial arts. Often called a *shillelagh*.

Bealtaine /bˈaltənˈə/ (I "May; first day of May") The beginning of summer in the Gaelic calendar, celebrated with a festival at the beginning of May, when the hawthorn trees bloom, or during the full moon closest to these events. The SG form of the name is *Bealltainn* /bˈaLtənˈ/.

Belenus /belenus/ (possibly from Gaulish **bel* "bright" or **belen* "intoxicating herb") Continental Celtic God, classically given solar connections, also known as Bel.

Beli Mawr /beli maur/ (W) Welsh ancestor figure, husband of Dôn and father to Arianrhod; possibly connected to Belenus and Bile.

Bile /bilə/ (OI) Irish ancestor figure associated with the Milesian invasion. Also the designation for a sacred tree in Irish tradition (often an Ash, Oak or Yew), under which royal inaugurations took place, along with other ceremonies and gatherings.

Bóann /boːəN/ (OI) Irish Goddess who created the eponymous River Boyne when She caused The Well of Wisdom to overflow and rush down to the sea. In the flood from the well, She is said to have lost an eye, arm and leg, which may symbolize that She is now halfway in this world, halfway in the Otherworld. As She brought the wisdom of the Other-world into the human world, She is now associated with poetic inspiration (though it is wisdom that may well come with a steep price). Associated with white cows, the Other-worldly wells of *Segais* and *Sídh Nechtán*, the fortress of *Brú na Bóinne* (Newgrange), and with the hazels and salmon of wisdom; She is also the mother of Oengus, resulting from Her liaison with the Dagda. Also known as Bóand, Boinn.

Boudicca /buːdikə/ (Brythonic) Historical queen of the Iceni tribe who, after the death of her husband, the rape of her daughters and her own flogging, refused the Roman claim on her people. She led a rebellion consisting of several tribes against the Romans in 61 C.E.

Bran /bran/ (W) aka Bendigeidfran, "Bran the Blessed," a royal figure from the *Mabinogi*, said to be of gigantic size, who raided Ireland to rescue his mistreated sister Branwen. He possessed a cauldron of rebirth. At the end of his tale, he is wounded and persists in life for 87 years as a head that continued to speak, until the head was finally interred in a hill to ward off future invasions of the Isle. He had other siblings, including Manawyddan fab Lyr, whose name is cognate to the Irish Manannán mac Lir.

Bran mac Febail /braːn mak fevəl´/ (I) Legendary pre-Christian king of Ireland who is the eponymous hero of *Immram Brain*, the earliest Irish voyage tale. In various related legends, his kingdom was flooded as the result of his Otherworld forays, and now lies beneath Loch Foyle in Northern Ireland.

Bricriu /br´ik´r´u/ (OI, possibly from *brecc* "speckled, freckled") aka Bricriu Nemthenga, "Bricriu the poison-tongued," a warrior, poet, and "troublemaker" from the Ulster Cycle of tales. Seen by some as trickster figure.

Bríde /br´iːd´ə/ (I) Irish and Scottish Goddess of healing, poetry and smithcraft; of sacred fire and holy wells, of inspiration, wisdom and knowledge. Also known as Brìghde, Brìde, Brighid, Brigid, Brigit. Possibly the tribal Goddess of the

Brigantes, a Brythonic group found on the Continent as well as in Scotland, England and eastern Ireland, and thus possibly related to the Goddess Brigantia commemorated in on a number of altars in England and Scotland. Her festival is Imbolc (*Lá Fhéile Bríde/Là Fhèill Brìghde*) at the beginning of February. She is also celebrated as a Christian saint.

Brighid See **Bríde**

Brythonic A group of the Celtic languages which includes Welsh, Breton, Cornish, and the extinct Cumbrian (of which only a few words survive). If Pictish is indeed an archaic Celtic language, it might also be classed among the Brythonic languages. Also found as "Brittonic."

Cailleach /kal´əx/ (SG "old woman, hag") Divine hag and creatrix. She created the mountain ranges of Scotland by striding across the land and dropping boulders from Her apron. In Scottish folklore She embodies the spirit of winter. She forms a seasonal duality, or dual Goddess, with Brìghde (Bríde), who represents the summer. In some Scottish tales She is known as Beira, and said to be the mother of all the Goddesses and Gods. There are numerous mountains and rocky cliffs dedicated to Her, in both Scotland and Ireland. The Scottish whirlpool of Corryvreckan (SG *Coirebhreacain*) is where She is said to usher in the winter by washing Her plaid until it is pure white and snow covers the land.

Cailleachan /kal´əxən/ (SG "old women") In Scotland, The Storm Hags, aka The Wind Hags – the personified forces of nature, especially when fierce and dangerous.

Cath Maige Tuired /kaθ mag´ə tur´əð´/ (OI "Battle of the Plain of Pillars") Important text in the Old Irish mythological cycle, also known as "The Second Battle of Moytura," in which the Túatha Dé Danann fight the Fomorians and are victorious in winning freedom for their people. Moytura is located in modern County Sligo, Ireland.

ceann /k´aN/ (I/SG "head") Used in much the same sense as the English word, including many of the same metaphoric associations.

cèilidh /kʹeːli/ (SG, pl. *cèilidhean* /kʹeːliən/) A concert of traditional Highland music; also used for a social visit. Originally meant a house-gathering at which tales were told, poetry recited, and music and songs shared.

Ceridwen /keridwen/ (W) Literary figure from the *Hanes Taliesin*, seen by some as a Goddess of inspiration and transformation. Variant spellings include Cerridwen, Ker(r)idwen.

Cín Dromma Snechtai /kʹiːn dromə sʹnʹextə/ (OI "Book of the Ridge of Snow") Oldest known Irish manuscript, from the monastery of Drumsnat in Co. Leitrim. Not now extant, but which is quoted in later manuscripts as being the source of such texts as *Immram Brain*, *Compert Con Culainn*, and for some of the doctrines of *Lebor Gabála Érenn*.

clann /kLaN/ (I/SG "children, offspring; race, descendants; followers") The group of descendants of a common ancestor and their retainers.

cleasa /kʹlʹasə/ (I "tricks; feats; knacks," sing. *cleas* /kʹlʹas/) Athletic activities which are engaged in by warriors to improve their combative abilities, or by anyone just for athletic accomplishment. Compare to *gaiscí*.

Coire Érmai /korʹə eːrʹəmʹə/ (OI "Cauldron of Motion"; I *Coire Éirime* /korʹə eːrʹəmʹə/) One of the three internal cauldrons discussed in the mystic poem known as "Cauldron of Poesy," said to be located in the chest, on its side within some people at birth, and which can be turned by sorrow or joy.

Coire Goiriath /korʹə gorʹəθ/ (OI "Cauldron of Warming"; I *Coire Gortha* /korʹə gorhə/) Another of the three internal cauldrons of the "Cauldron of Poesy" poem, located in the belly and considered "upright" in every healthy person.

Coire Sofhis /korʹə soəs/ (OI "Cauldron of Wisdom"; I *Coire Sofheasa* /korʹə soasə/) The third of the cauldrons discussed in the mystic poem, "Cauldron of Poesy," located in the head and turned "on its lips" (i.e. upside-down) in everyone at birth, but which through poetic training can be turned upright.

Coligny calendar Gaulish solar and lunar calendar.

córrguineacht /koːrgunˈəxt/ (OI "crane-magic" or "crane-wounding") A type of magical curse, performed by Lugh during the great battle of Magh Tuiredh, in which one assumes a one-legged stance and a one-eyed visage, while reciting a particularly virulent satire known as the *glam dícenn*.

CR Acronym/abbreviation for "Celtic Reconstructionism," "Celtic Reconstructionist" as well as "Celtic Reconstructionist Paganism."

crannogham /kraNoːm/ (I "tree *ogham*" also *crann ogham*) The *ogham* of trees, where each letter/glyph is assigned to a different type of tree. See **ogham**.

Creidne /krʹeðʹnʹə/ (OI) The daughter of Conall Costamail, a king of Ulster, who was raped by him and then exiled into the wilderness along with the three sons she bore him. They were liminal as she and her sons had no "proper" social roles due her being both daughter and unwilling consort to her father, and the boys being simultaneously his sons and grandsons. This also made Creidne and her sons "rivals" to his official wife and her sons. Creidne became a *banfénnid* – a woman member of a *fianna* war band – and led the band in attacks against her father's troops until she forced him to acknowledge her rights and those of her sons, then she and her sons rejoined society.

Cú Chulainn /kuː xulənʹ/ (OI "Hound of Cualu") Hero of the Old Irish Ulster Cycle, son of the God Lugh and the mortal woman Dechtine/Dechtire, sister of the Ulster king Conchobor mac Nessa. He was reputed to have been conceived three times and born twice. He is the principal protagonist of the epic *Táin Bó Cúailnge* as well as many other tales, and renowned as the greatest warrior of ancient Ireland.

Dagda /dayðə/ (OI *dag* "good" + *dia* "god") One of the principal Irish Gods and chieftains of the Túatha Dé Danann. Associated with abundance and knowledge, and the possessor of many skills. The "good" God not necessarily in a moral sense, but in that He is seen to be "good" or "skilled" at everything He puts His hand to. Variant form Daghda.

Danu /dɑːnu/ (OI) Tutelary Goddess and mother of the Túatha Dé Danann. Seen by some as synonymous with Anu, while others see Them as two separate, though related, Goddesses. Considered by some CRs to be particularly connected to the land and to rivers.

Daoine-Sìth /duːnˈə sˈiː/ (SG "peaceful people, people of the mounds") The "fairy folk" of Scotland; the spirits who dwell in the fairy mounds. In various sources, the spirits of the Otherworlds, the spirits of nature, the ancestors, or the Celtic Deities in a later, literary form. The use of this euphemism ("peaceful") and others like it, such as "the good neighbors," is based on the belief that if we speak kindly of the spirits they may in turn be kind to us. Also written *Daoine Sìdh* which, while less common, is also correct. Both spellings have the same meaning and pronunciation. See also **Síd**, **Sídhe** and **Aos Sí**.

Déithe /dˈeːhə/ (I "gods; deities," sing. *dia* /dˈiə/) Gods, specifically the Gods of the Gaelic peoples.

Dian Cécht /dˈiən kˈeːxt/ (OI) Túatha Dé Danann God of healing and prosthetic medicine. Murdered His son Miach in jealousy when Miach surpassed Him in surgical skill, and attempted to ruin His daughter's cataloguing of the healing herbs. Grandfather of Lugh via His son Cian. See **Airmid**.

diaspora An ethnic group that has been dispersed or driven from their original homelands. "The Celtic diaspora" refers to people of Celtic heritage who are now living outside of the six Celtic nations.

Dichetal do chennaib /diːxˈedəl do xˈeNəvˈ/ (OI "reciting from heads") One of the "three things required of a poet," which was allowed in Irish law to continue into the Christian period according to legal sources on poetry, interpreted by most scholars as extemporaneous poetic composition or improvisation.

dindshenchas /dˈinhenəxəs/ (OI "lore of important places") Collection of place-name lore, from which many important mythological tales concerning Bóann, Macha, and other Deities and ancestors are drawn.

Dôn /doːn/ (W) Welsh ancestor Goddess, cognate with the Irish Danu, mother of figures including Amaethon, Arianrhod, Gilvaethwy, Gofannon and Gwydion.

Domnu /dovnu/ (OI) The ancestral mother Goddess of the Fomorians (aka the Túatha Dé Domnann). Possibly a primal Goddess of the deep ocean, and the peoples of the ocean, the way Danu and/or Anu are seen as the primal mothers of the Túatha Dé Danann. Some CRs believe Danu, Domnu and Anu together make a triad of the primal Goddesses of the Three Realms – Land, Sea and Sky.

draoí /driː/ (I "druid; wizard, magician; diviner; trickster," pl. *draoithe* /driːhə/) A druid. The SG form of the word is *draoidh* /druːi/, pl. *draoidhean* /druːiən/, and in OI it is *druí* /drui/, pl. *druid* /druið/.

Epona /epoː na/ (Gaulish) Goddess associated with horses, whose name is connected to one of the primary roots for "horse" in the Celtic languages (**ekwos*, giving *ech* in Irish, *ebol* in Welsh, etc.). Seen by many as a cognate to the Irish Goddess Macha and the Welsh Goddess Rhiannon, as well as possibly the Irish Roech (*ro-ech*, "super-horse"), who was the mother of Fergus.

Ériu /erʹu/ (OI) One of three Goddesses of Ireland who agreed to allow the Milesians to land on the island. Her name is most familiar as synonymous with Ireland, and the Old and Modern Irish words for the island are all derived from Her personal name. See **Banba** and **Fótla**.

Esus /eːsus/ (Gaulish) In Lucan's *Pharsalia*, one of the principle Gods of Gaul, along with Taranis and Teutates (though not considered as prominent in other sources). Depicted on an altar and a relief sculpture as a youthful woodsman cutting a tree.

FAQ Acronym/abbreviation for "Frequently Asked Questions." On the Internet, a file of information to help newcomers learn basic facts about a subject. The information is usually presented in a question and answer format – oddly enough, the same format used in such medieval Irish texts as the prose *dindshenchas* as well as some legal texts.

fáidh /faːi/ (I "prophet; wise man, sage," pl. *fáithe* /faːh′ə/) A diviner. Cognate with the Brythonic term *ovate* and the Gaulish term *vate*.

fáilte /faːlt′ə/ (I "welcome") Common Gaelic greeting; the SG form is *fàilte* /faːlt′ə/. A common variant of this is I *céad míle fáilte* /k′eːd m′iːlə f′aːlt′e/, SG *ceud mile fàilte* /kiad miːlə faːlt′e/ "a hundred thousand welcomes."

Fairy Faith In the Celtic lands and the diaspora, the living tradition of belief in, and interaction with, the spirits of nature and the Otherworlds. Generally practiced by simple offerings to the spirits, awareness of their role in the world, and avoiding offending them by respecting nature, certain taboos and their particular abodes.

Fand /faːnð/ (OI "tear") Goddess of the upper sea and Otherworldly islands, associated with *Tír Tairngiri* ("the Land of Promise") and *Tír na mBan* ("the Isle of Women"). Appears in the tale *Serglige Con Culainn* ("The Wasting Sickness of Cú Chulainn"), initially in the form of a sea bird attached by a gold chain to Her sister, Lí Ban ("Splendor of Women," also in bird form). After Cú Chulainn throws stones at the birds/Goddesses, Fand and Lí Ban appear as "Otherworldly women" and whip him almost to death with horsewhips, causing him to lie abed for a year. Said to be the most beautiful of Goddesses, associated by many with healing and pleasure, but known to punish those who offend Her or Her creatures.

Faobhar Chleas /fiːvər x′l′as/ (I "edge feat") The Feat of the Sword-Edge. A war-dance engaged in prior to combat, both to warm up and to intimidate opponents.

Fear-Sgliùrachan Fànais /fer sgl′urəxən faːnəs′/ (SG "Man-Whores from Outer Space") See **Man-Whores from Outer Space**.

fianna /f′iəNə/ (OI "warrior-hunters," sing. *fiann* /f′iəN/) Groups of youthful warriors in a pre-adult, "Outsider" phase, associated with heat, hunting, liminality, dogs/wolves, and the wilderness.

fidlanna /f′iðlaNə/ (OI "divination by wood") A rare word from the apocalyptic Christian text *Adomnán's Second Vision* which, in comparison to other Old Irish sources, seems to indicate a form of divination which involved the use of some sort of wooden pieces.

fidnemed /f'iðnev'əð'/ (OI) A "woodland sanctuary."

filí See *file*.

file /f'ilə/ (I "poet," pl. *filí* /f'ili:/; SG *filidh* /f'ili/, pl. *filidhean* /f'iliən/; OI *fili* /f'il'ə/, pl. *filid* /f'iləð'/) The Old Irish *filid* were professional poets, seers, storytellers and lore-keepers, with additional duties that appear to have included divination, magic, tradition-keeping, and social constraint through praise and satire. Cognate with the Norse *völva* and the Old Germanic *veleda*.

filidecht /f'il'ið'əxt/ (OI "poetry, divination, the art of poetry"; I *filíocht* /f'il'i:əxt/; SG *filidheachd* /f'iliəxk/, though in modern SG *bàrdachd* /ba:rdaxk/ is more commonly used) In a spiritual sense, used to refer to a system of devotional, poetic mysticism, in which the practice of poetry is interwoven with methods of seeking vision, inspiration, and communion with the Deities and spirits.

filíocht /f'il'i:(ə)xt/ (I "poetry") See *filidecht*.

fiodh /f'iə/ (I "tree, wood, stick," pl. *feánna* /f'a:Nə/) Generally used to refer to a piece of wood on which an *ogham* letter/glyph has been drawn. The SG form is *fiodh* /f'iəɣ/ (and in the modern language means "wood, timber" as a material, thus no pl. form); the OI form is *fid* /f'ið'/, pl. *feda* /f'eðə/. See also *ogham* and *fidlanna*.

fiodh-naomheadh /f'iə ni:v'ə/ (I "woodland sanctuary") See *fidnemed*.

Fionn mac Cumhaill /f'iəN mac ku:əl'/ (SG/I) Warrior-poet, leader of the *fianna*, and hero of an eponymous literary cycle (sometimes called the Ossianic Cycle, after his famous son Oisín). The tales of Fionn and the *fianna* have early roots in Irish literature, and became quite widespread in the post-medieval tradition and oral storytelling. The stories have been particularly popular in Scotland, largely due to the romantic pseudo-archaism of James MacPherson's *Ossian*.

Fir Bolg /fʹir boləg / (OI) In the *Lebor Gabála Érenn*, the peoples who arrived in Ireland in the last wave of invasions before the arrival of the Túatha Dé Danann, and who were later defeated by the Túatha Dé Danann at the first battle of Magh Tuiredh. Generally seen as Deities or ancestral spirits particularly connected with the earth and agriculture, they survive in Scottish folklore as fairy folk who are said to live in caves. Historically, it is possible the Fir Bolg are based upon earlier P-Celtic peoples who were later absorbed or displaced by the Q-Celtic peoples.

fír fer /fʹiːr fʹer/ (OI "truth of men") Ethical concept present in many Irish tales, concerning "fair play" and equality in combat.

fír flatha /fʹiːr flaθə/ (OI "truth of rulers") Idealized rulership/sovereignty in ancient Ireland, reflecting the rightful ruler's ability to speak truthful and binding judgments, and the entire relationship with the Otherworld which allows peace and agricultural plenty to occur.

Fomorian /fomoriːən/ (I *Fomhórach* /fovoːrəx/ "giant"; pl. *Fomhóraigh* /fovoːri/) Older tribe of Deities or ancestral spirits, largely seen as the foes of the Túatha Dé Danann, though many of the later Irish Deities were part Fomorian (e.g. Lugh) or fostered by Fomorian parents. People of the Goddess Domnu, associated with the sea, the underworld, and the Outsiders.

Fótla /foːdlə/ (OI) Ancient Irish Goddess who agreed with Amairgen to allow the Milesians to land on the island. See **Ériu** and **Banba**.

forfeda /foːrfeðə/ (OI "additional woods") The five additional *ogham* letters that were added much later in the manuscripts, probably in an effort on the part of scribes to bring the alphabet more in line with Latin and Greek. Very rarely, if ever, found on the *ogham* stones.

Gaeilge /geːlʹgʹə/ The Irish name for the Irish Gaelic language (aka "Irish"). /geːlʹgʹə/ is the pronunciation in Connemara dialects, which was taken into the literary standard; southern dialects have the pronunciation /geːliŋ/ and northern dialects have /ge:lək´/, whence the usual English pronunciation of the word "Gaelic."

Gaelic   Of or pertaining to the Gaels, their culture, or their language. Historically, the Gaelic world (Ireland, Scotland, and the Isle of Man) was united linguistically and culturally; in modern times, the three Gaelic nations are generally politically and linguistically distinct from each other. In reference to the language, the modern Irish and Manx varieties are usually referred to simply as "Irish" and "Manx," rather than as "Gaelic"; while in Scotland, Scottish Gaelic is referred to simply as "Gaelic." In Scotland it is pronounced "gahllik" (from the SG *Gàidhlig*) rather than "gaylik." However, it is worth noting that these differences exist in English only; in all varieties of Gaelic, the name of the language is still simply "Gaelic" (I *Gaeilge*, SG *Gàidhlig*, Manx *Gaelg*).

Gaeltacht /ge:ltəxt/   (I, pl. *Gaeltachtaí* /ge:ltəxti:/)   An area in Ireland where Irish is still spoken.

Gàidhealtachd /ge:əLtaxk/   (SG, pl. *Gàidhealtachdan* /ge:əLtaxkən/) Though it literally means "Gaelic-speaking area," like the Irish *Gaeltacht*, the word in Scottish Gaelic usually refers to the Highlands of Scotland, which were historically Gaelic in language and culture, but mostly English-speaking today. There is thus some ambiguity in modern usage, as the word is also sometimes used to refer to the area(s) where Gaelic is still spoken, notably the Western Isles. The word is also sometimes used to refer to the Scottish Gaelic-speaking community in Cape Breton, Nova Scotia.

Gàidhlig /ga:lək´/   (SG) The Scottish Gaelic name for the Scottish Gaelic language.

gaiscí /gas´k´i:/   (I "arms, weapons," sing. *gaisce* /gas´k´ə/) Techniques directly related to fighting. Derived from OI *gaisced,* "weapons," a compound of *gae* "spear" and *sciath* "shield," which were a warrior's basic equipment. Compare to **cleasa.**

gaoithe /gi:hə/   (I "winds," sing. *gaoth* /gi:/) The SG equivalents are sing. *gaoth* /guː/, pl. *gaothean* /guːən/.

geasa See *geis*.

geis /g´es´/ (I "taboo, prohibition, binding injunction, spell, charm," pl. *geasa* /g´esə/) Taboo or ritual prohibition, the following of which can bring power, the breaking of which can result in death or similar calamity. The SG forms are sing. *geas* /g´es/, pl. *geasan* /g´esən/; OI *geis* /g´es´/, pl. *gessi* /g´esi/.

Glam Dícenn /gLa:v d´i:g´eN/ (OI *glam* "satire" and *dícenn* "extreme or utmost") A poetic curse performed on one leg with one hand behind the back and one eye closed, imitative of the posture of a crane, often used in battle for destroying the enemy. Also known as *córrguinneacht*. Alternately, a metrical poetic satire intended to harm by raising blisters and marks on the face. The name of the satire implies that it is the most extreme action that a poet can take.

glanadh /gLanə/ (I "cleaning, clearance"; SG *glanadh* /gLanəɣ/)

Goibhniu /gov´n´u/ (OI *gobae* "smith") Smith and armourer of the Túatha Dé Danann. One of a trio of such Gods (the others being Credne the brazier and Luchta the carpenter), referred to in some tales as the "three Gods of skill" (*trí dé dána*). He is mentioned in an Old Irish spell as a God invoked to assist in the removal of a thorn.

Grían /g´r´iən/ (OI "sun") Goddess worshipped in the South of Ireland, possibly the sister of Áine. She has a sacred hill near that of Áine. Some believe the two sisters are represented by the "two suns" of the year – Áine the strong, red sun of summer (I *an ghrian mhór*; SG *a' ghrian mhòr*) and Grian the weaker, white sun of winter (I *an ghrian bheag*; SG *a' ghrian bheag*).

Gwydion /gwədyon/ (Welsh) Character from the *Mabinogi* who excels in magic, warfare and storytelling, who assists his nephew/possible son Llew Llaw Gyffes to gain his name and arms from his mother Arianrhod, and with his uncle Math creates Llew's wife Blodeuedd.

Gwynn ap Nudd /gwi:n ap ni:ð/ (W, from *gwyn* "white, fair") Warrior associated with the Welsh Annwfn or the Otherworld. Exact linguistic cognate of the Irish Fionn mac

Cumhaill (who was a descendant of the Irish Nuada, likely identical with the God of the same name and cognate to Nudd), probably sharing a common source in an insular Celtic Deity called *Windos.

House of Donn Sea stack/island off the southwest coast of Ireland, where the dead are believed to go; now called the Bull (with its nearby neighbors, the Cow and the Calf) off the Bearra Peninsula, Co. Cork. Perhaps where the dead pause before journeying west to the Isles of the Dead. Others believe the dead head immediately to the west, and do not stay in the House of Donn. See *Teach Duinn.*

Ildiachas Atógtha /il'd'iəxəs atoːkə/ (I "rebuilt/reconstructed polytheism") A specific CR sub-tradition, founded by C. Lee Vermeers.

imbas /imbəs/ (OI) See *iomas.*

imbas forosnai /imbəs foːroːsni/ (OI "great knowledge which illuminates") One of the "three things required of a poet," which Fionn mac Cumhaill was said to have gained as the result of eating the Salmon of Wisdom. Usually interpreted by scholars as "inspiration," i.e. the supernatural connection with the source of all poetry and art. Also the name of a ritual described in *Sanas Cormaic* which involves an incubation after several liminality-inducing actions are undertaken.

Imbolc /imoləg/ (I/SG) Festival at the beginning of February, sacred to the Goddess Bríde/Brìghde. aka *Lá Fhéile Bríde* in Ireland and *Là Fhèill Brìghde* in Scotland.

immram /imrəv/ (OI "rowing around," pl. *immrama* /imrəvə/) Archaic word for a sea voyage, used in the old tales to refer to magical, Otherworldly journeys to various enchanted or supernatural islands. Sometimes used among CRs to refer to Otherworld journeying and visionary work involving a marine or oceanic Otherworld. In modern I and SG, *iomramh* /imrəv/, pl. *iomraimh* /imrəv'/, is the common, everyday word for "rowing." Variant forms of the word in SG include *iomradh* and *iomairt.*

iomas /iməs/ (I "intuition") Poetic inspiration, associated with fire. Often seen as fire arising from water, or fire arising from one's head. Believed by some CRs to be the primal fire (or fiery water) of creation and the creative impulse. Closely associated, therefore, with the Goddesses Bríde and Bóann. Modern Irish spelling of *imbas*.

Lá Bealtaine /La: bˊaltənˊə/ (I "the day of May") The first day of May. A festival marking the beginning of summer. The SG form is *Là Bealltainn* /La: bˊaLtənˊ/, also *Là Buidhe Bealltainn* /La: buɣˊə bˊaLtənˊ/ "the lucky day of Beltane" (literally "the yellow day of Beltane," yellow being the color traditionally associated with luck or good fortune in Gaelic culture).

Lá Fhéile Bríde /La: eːlˊə briːdˊə/ (I "the day of the festival of Bríde") The first day of February. A festival sacred to the Goddess Bríde, aka Imbolc. The SG form is *Là Fhèill Brìghde* /La: eːlˊ brˊiːdˊə/.

Lá Lúnasa /La: luːnəsə/ (I "the day of August") The first day of August. A festival marking the beginning of the harvest in some areas, often the ripening of the berries. Traditionally a time of family gatherings and community festivals. The SG form is *Lùnastal/Lùnasdal* /LuːnəstəL/ (which in modern SG is usually encountered as the name for the month of August as a whole).

Latha na Cailliche /laː(hə) nə kailˊixˊə/ (SG "day of the Cailleach, day of the Hag") Scottish festival celebrated on or around March 25; seen in colder bioregions as the day the Cailleach's reign over winter finally gives way to Brìde's reign over summer. It is also sometimes a festival for the Cailleachan (the Storm Hags) as a group, as in some areas they are still raising the spring storms at this time (the last burst of wintry weather, usually at the beginning of March, is known as *A' Chailleach*). Variations in local, seasonal weather patterns also result in the Cailleachan being honored, petitioned, or bargained with whenever storms threaten, such as during hurricane season for those on the coasts. (In *The Silver Bough*, F. Marian McNeill calls the holiday "*Latha na Cailleach*, the Auld Wife's Day"; however, the correct form for "Day of the Cailleach" is *Latha na Cailliche*. Sometimes in informal speech the final "e" is dropped, giving *Latha na Caillich* /la:(hə) nə kail'ix'/. "Day of the Storm Hags" can be written either *Latha nan Cailleach* or *Latha nan Cailleachan.*)

Lebor Gabála Érenn /l'ev'ər gav'a:lə e:r'ən / (OI "Book of the Taking of Ireland") Pseudohistorical work detailing the various invasions of Ireland, beginning with the descendants of Cesair, then Partholón (sometimes followed by an invasion of the *Conchennaig*), then Nemed, then the Fir Bolg, the Túatha Dé Danann, and finally the Milesians.

líon tí /l'i:n t'i:/ (I "household, family," lit. "the full complement of a house")

Llew Llaw Gyffes /ɬeu ɬaw gəfes/ (W) Figure in the fourth branch of the *Mabinogi* and generally considered the Welsh cognate of Lugh.

Lugh /Lu:/ (I, OI form *Lug* /Lu:ɣ/, etymology uncertain) Chief of the Túatha Dé Danann and a prominent hero of Irish tradition and mythology.

Lúnasa /lu:nəsə/ (I "August") Sometimes used to refer to the festival of *Lá Lúnasa.*

Mabinogi /mabinogi/ (W "The Four Branches of the Mabinogi," aka *Pedeir Keinc y Mabinogi* /pedeir keiŋk ə mabinogi/) The primary medieval Welsh mythological narrative. The four branches are called *Pwyll Pendeuic Dyfet, Branwen verch Lyr, Manawydan fab Llyr,* and *Math vab Mathonwy.* Characters including Rhiannon, Arawn, Llew, Gwydion, Bran, Arianrhod, and others appear in these inter-related texts.

Mabon /mabon/ (W "divine son") This is the name of a Welsh mythic figure, a great hunter and one of the "famous prisoners of Britain," cognate with the Continental/Brythonic Deity Maponos, and known from the Welsh Triads and the Arthurian tale *Culhwch ac Olwen.* Though sometimes used as such by Neopagans, it is not the name of any holiday or festival.

Macha /maxə/ (I possibly "plain") Warrior Goddess from the Ulster region, especially connected with Armagh (Ard Mhacha), Eamhain Mhacha, Oenach Mhacha and Magh

Mhacha. She is associated with sovereignty, the land, war and horses. There are at least three definably separate Machas, two of them offering different origins to the name Eamhain Macha. Although complex Herself, She is also considered a part of or connected to the Morrígan. One of the Machas, when mistreated by the rulers of Ulster, cursed the Ulstermen to be stricken with labour pains in their hour of greatest need. This rendered the Ulstermen unable to fight in the Cattle Raid of Cooley. Another Macha ruled as a queen after defeating the other claimants to the throne (all men) in physical combat.

Manannán mac Lir /manana:n mak l'ir'/ (OI) Sea God who appears frequently in the cycles of Irish literature and traditions, with His earliest appearance being in *Immram Brain*. He often travels over the waves in His chariot or on horseback. He is able to cast spells and taught this skill to the druids. He possesses a cloak of mists and was said to have been the first king of the Isle of Man. Many CRs see Him as a Deity of the mists between worlds and a psychopomp.

Man-Whores from Outer Space Seminal CR glam rock band. Rumoured to have ghostwritten the CR FAQ. aka *Fear-Sgliùrachan Fànais*.

Maponos /maponos/ (Gaulish, Romano-British) "Divine youth" worshipped in ancient Gaul and commemorated on altars in Celtic Britain, where He is connected with Apollo as a God of music. Likely related to the Welsh Mabon and the Irish Oengus Mac ind Óc.

Medb /meðəv/ (OI "one who intoxicates"; I *Meadhbh* /m'e:v/, Anglicized Maeve) A sovereignty Goddess of Connacht, euhemerized as the Connacht queen who initiated the *Táin Bó Cúailnge* ("Cattle Raid of Cooley") by stealing a bull in order to try to best the one Her husband possessed.

Milesians (Anglicized Irish) The descendants of Míl Espaine ("Spanish soldier"), the first ancestor of the Gaelic populations of Ireland. His career places him in both Scythia and as a servant of the Egyptian pharaoh Nectanebus, and his children Donn and Amairgen eventually settle Ireland after defeating the Túatha Dé Danann.

An Mhor-Ríoghain /ən vor riːən/ or /ən wor riːən/ (I "The Phantom Queen"; sometimes rendered as *An Mhór-Ríoghain* /an voːr riːən/ or /an woːr riːən/ "The Great Queen") Triple Goddess of battle, sovereignty and prophecy, known in Old Irish as *An Morrígan.* Primarily associated with crows, though in the epic *Táin Bó Cúailnge* She also appeared in the form of a red cow, a grey wolf, and an eel. As a sovereignty Goddess, She demonstrated the power to grant victory in battle to those who earn Her favor (see **Dagda**) and to bring defeat and death to those who offend Her (see **Cú Chulainn**). Though the primary sources do vary on this point, Her triadic manifestations are most often considered to be the Goddesses Macha, Badb and Nemain. See **An Morrígan.**

An Morrígan /moriːɣən/ (OI "phantom queen") Goddess of war fury in early Irish tradition, usually spoken of with the definite article, "the Morrígan." As one Goddess, also sometimes referred to as "The Morrigu" and, when present as three separate Goddesses, by the plural form, An Morrígna. See **An Mhor-Ríoghain.**

naomheadh /niːvˊə/ Modern Irish spelling of *nemed.*

nemed /neveð/ (OI "sacred, holy, sanctuary") Usually used to refer to a particular sanctuary, grove or temple, whether ancient or contemporary; also used in legal texts for the "privileged" classes in society (i.e. nobility, the skilled and the learned). A legendary leader of the third invasion of Ireland was also named Nemed; he and his followers fought the Fomorians.

nemeton /nemeton/ (Gaulish) "Sacred grove, sanctuary."

Nigheanan nan Cailleachan /nˊiːənən nən kalˊəxən/ (SG "Daughters of the Storm Hags," or, lit. "Daughters of the Old Women") A CR women's group and family tradition, co-founded by Kathryn Price NicDhàna and other frightening members of her family.

Nuada /nuəðə/ (I) Irish king of the Túatha Dé Danann, who after the first battle of Moytura lost his arm and had it replaced with a silver one by Dian Cécht, then later with one of flesh by Miach and Airmid.

Oengus Mac ind Óc /oingəs mac ən oːg/ (OI, variant spelling *Aenghus*) Son of Bóann and the Dagda, associated with the Otherworld fortress of Newgrange (*Brú na Bóinne*), and *deus ex machina* of many Irish tales. Cognate to the Welsh Mabon and the Gaulish Maponos.

ogham /oːm/ (I; OI *ogam* /oɣəm/; SG *ogham* /oəm/) A cipher or alphabet developed in the 3ʳᵈ or 4ᵗʰ century C.E. in Southwest Ireland. Surviving inscriptions are on stone and occasionally bone, but lore mentions it also having been carved on wood. Later it was documented in manuscripts such as *The Book of Ballymote*. Used by many CRs as a system for meditation, magic, divination, and various methods of omen-seeking. A related spelling in SG, *oidheam* or *oigheam*, means "a secret meaning." See also *fidlanna*.

ogham fiodh See *fiodh*.

Oghma /oːmə/ (I; OI *Ogma*) Warrior champion of the Túatha Dé Danann as well as the inventor of the *ogham* alphabet. Cognate to a warrior God and God of eloquence in Gaul called Ogmios.

Oíche Shamhna /iːx′ə haunə/ (I "night of Samhain"; SG *Oidhche Shamhna* /əix′ə haunə/) See **Samhain**.

ollamh /oLəv/ (I "master-poet, doctor") The highest poetic grade among ancient poets. In modern Irish usage, someone with a doctorate, or in academia, someone who has attained the rank of full professor.

Pàganachd /paːgənəxk/ (SG "Paganism, Heathenism") Used by some CRs to specifically indicate traditional Gaelic polytheism.

Pàganachd Bhandia /paːgənəxk vand′iə/ (SG "Paganism of Goddesses," or "Goddesses' Paganism") A specific CR sub-tradition focused on the Gaelic Goddesses, founded by Kathryn Price NicDhàna.

Págántacht /paːgaːntəxt/ (I "Paganism, Heathenism." Variant, but less common, form: **Págánacht** /paːgaːnəxt/) See **Pàganachd**.

P-Celtic The Celtic linguistic group including the Brythonic languages (Welsh, Breton, Cornish and Cumbrian, and possibly Pictish) as well as the Continental Celtic languages of Cisalpine Gaulish (from Northern Italy), Transalpine Gaulish (Switzerland, France, and southern Germany), Lepontic (from Northern Italy) and Galatian (in modern Turkey). P-Celtic languages are distinguished by their rendering of the proto-Indo-European sound *kw- as p, as demonstrated in the Welsh word for "son," map, and pen, "head." See also **Q-Celtic**.

pen /pen/ (W "head") See *ceann*.

Q-Celtic The Celtic linguistic group including the Goidelic languages (Irish, Scottish Gaelic, and Manx) as well as the Continental Celtiberian language recorded in parts of modern Spain. Q-Celtic languages are distinguished by their rendering of the proto-Indo-European sound *kw- as q and eventually c, as demonstrated in the Irish word for "son," given in *Ogham* Irish as MAQQI and Old Irish as *mac*. See also **P-Celtic**.

Rhiannon /Rianon/ Welsh Goddess found in the *Mabinogi*, associated with sovereignty, horses, and Otherworldly birds whose songs soothe the hearers.

Rosmerta /rosmurtə/ (Gaulish) Goddess often paired with the Gaulish "Mercury" (a form of Lugus, the Gaulish Lugh or Llew) in reliefs, connected to fertility, fortune, and possibly war.

saining /seːniŋ/ (Sc "blessing, sanctifying, consecrating," from verb *sain* /seːn/) Traditional Scots name for ritual acts involving blessing and protection. From the Early Irish *sén*, "blessing, sign, luck." Used to describe the action of blessing an area or person with the fire and smoke of burning peat, torches, candles or purifying herbs (usually juniper), or similar actions accomplished with water. In Scots, Irish, and Scottish Gaelic forms also refers to the use of protective charms and incantations, as well as those for good luck.

Samhain /saun´/ (I "month of November"; SG *Samhain* /savən´/ or /sawən´/ "November, Hallowtide, All Souls Day," alternate spellings *Samhainn, Samhuinn*; OI *Samain* /savən´/

"end of summer") The beginning of winter in the Gaelic calendar, celebrated with a festival at the beginning of November, or at the local occurrence of first frost. Usually a festival dedicated to the ancestors. Generally regarded as the "Celtic New Year," though it is not certain if it was seen as such in antiquity.

samos/giamos (Proto-Celtic "light half/dark half of the year," "summer/winter") The division of the year, marked by Bealtaine and Samhain. The light half was considered a time of active, open activities and energy, while the dark half was of inactive and hidden ones.

Scáthach /ska:həx/ (I "shadowy") Legendary warrior woman and martial arts teacher, said to live on an island in the North of Scotland (perhaps the Isle of Skye). Particularly famed as the teacher/foster-mother of Cú Chulainn and his foster-brother/adversary Fear Diadh.

Scots Language Sister language of English, descended from northern dialects of Anglo-Saxon and spoken mostly in the lowlands of Scotland, though it is also found to some degree in Ulster (where it was brought by Protestant settlers from Scotland) and in some areas of England and Ireland. Not to be confused with Scottish Gaelic! Variant names abound for regional dialects of Scots, e.g. *Doric* (Northeast Scots), *The Patter* (Glaswegian Scots), and *Shetlandic* (Shetland Scots). The term *Lallans* is occasionally found – derived from the word *Lawlan(d)s* "Lowlands," it refers to a literary variety of Scots created in the 20th century and promulgated in a periodical of the same name. The name *Ullans*, modeled after *Lallans*, may be encountered for Ulster Scots.

seisiún /s'es'u:n/ (I "session, social gathering," pl. *seisiúin* /s'es'un'/) Usually used in reference to informal gatherings of Irish traditional musicians, to play traditional music. Often held in pubs. May also include poetry, storytelling and conversation.

shameon (i.e. "shame on") A fraudulent shaman, aka "plastic medicine (wo)man." Someone who is exploiting, misappropriating, and/or misrepresenting indigenous religion. Colloquial pejorative, originating in the Native

American/First Nations communities, also applied to others engaging in cultural appropriation or newage (rhymes with "sewage") scams. A similar term, "plastic paddy," is sometimes used to refer to those who misappropriate or misrepresent Irish culture.

síd(h) /s´i:ð/ (OI "burial mound," "fairy hill," "fairy mound" pl. *síde* /s´i:ð´ə/; I *sí* /s´i:/, pl. *síthe* /s´i:hə/; SG *sìthean* /s´i:(h)an/, pl. *sìtheananan* /s´i:(h)anən/) An earthen mound (often an ancient tomb) where the *Aos Sí*, or *Daoine-Sìth*, are believed to live. *Síd* is also the Old Irish word for "peace" (SG *sìth* /s´i:/; I *síocháin* /s´i:xa:n´/), which was imagined to have its source in the divine Otherworld. In singular or plural, only used to refer to the mounds, never simply to the people.

síd(h)e /s´i:ð´ə/ (OI "of a/the fairy mound") In some English-language sources, the fairy folk are sometimes referred to simply as "the *Sídhe*," but in Gaelic this is incorrect. This oft-reproduced mistake probably resulted from English-speakers' attempts to abbreviate the Old Irish phrase *Áes Síde, Áes Sídhe*, or similar nomenclature for "the people of the mounds," without an understanding of Gaelic grammar. In actual Gaelic usage, only the mounds are called *síd(h)e, síthe* or *sìtheananan*, while the spirits who inhabit the mounds are referred to as "the people of the mounds" – *Aos Sí* or *Daoine-Sìth*. Occasionally in SG (as in MacBain) you will find *sìth* given a secondary meaning of "a fairy," but far more often the words for "a fairy" are *sióg* (I pl. *sióga*) and *sìdhiche/sìthiche* (SG pl. *sìdhichean/sìthichean*). In both Scottish Gaelic and Irish, *sí/sìdh/sìth* is also used as an adjective to modify nouns, resulting in terms such as *bean sí* ("fairy woman/woman of the sí") and *an slua sí* ("the fairy host"), among numerous others.

Tailltiu /tal´d´u:/ (OI) Early Irish Goddess, who died of exhaustion after clearing the plains of Ireland for agriculture. Fir Bolg Goddess of the earth and harvest, celebrated at the August festival of *Lá Lúnasa*. Foster-mother of Lugh, who instituted funeral games in Her honor. Also the name of one of the major assemblies held in August. Also known as Tailtiu, Tailte, Taillte.

Táin Bó Cúailnge /ta:n′ bo: ku:ələŋ′ə/ (OI "Cattle Raid of Cooley") Centerpiece of the Irish Ulster Cycle, in which the Goddess Medb seeks a supernatural bull held on the Cooley Peninsula of modern Co. Louth, and gathers an army from all of Ireland to do so, with the Ulster exile and former king Fergus mac Roich assisting. Ulster is defended from Samhain to Imbolc single-handedly by Cú Chulainn, and eventually the Ulstermen rise from the curse of Macha to rebuff the offensive. The two great bulls kill each other, with Donn Cúailnge ("the Brown of Cooley") winning against his Connacht rival before his final death; in their combat, the two shape the landscape and strew their anatomy across it, giving its features names, until the Donn's "heart bursts from bellowing" and he plunges into a lake at his death.

Tara (I) Anglicized form of the ritual center of Ireland in the Skrene Valley of Co. Meath; the Old Irish form is *Temair* (gen. *Temrach* or *Temro*). Site of two hundred estimated archaeological sites which are crucial to Irish history.

Taranis /taranis/ (Gaulish, related to Welsh and Breton *taran* and Irish *toirneach*, "thunder") Continental Celtic thunder and sky God whose worship was found from Celtic Britain to the Balkans. Usually depicted with a wheel.

tarbhfheis /tarəv′es′/ (I "bull feast") A divinatory ritual which involved the seer gorging on the meat of a sacrificed bull then wrapping up in the bull skin to enter a trance. Known primarily as a method of choosing the Irish high king of Tara.

Teach Duinn /t′ax dun′/ (I "House of Donn") Otherworld island in the southwest, where the dead reside under the leadership of Donn, who may be a God of the Dead and/or the first ancestor of the Milesians to die in Ireland. See **House of Donn**.

teach an allais /t′ax ən aLəs′/ (I "sweat house"; SG *taigh an fhallais* /taɣ′ ən aLəs′/; given in Martin Martin as *tigh 'n alluis*) Gaelic sweat house. Small structures built of stone, historically found in Gaelic areas. Lore has it they were used as a type of sauna, in at least some cases also involving prayer and contemplation while sweating.

Teutates /tuːtaːteːs/ (Gaulish) Gaulish God whose name fundamentally means "God of the Tribe" (cognate with Irish *tuath*).

The Three Realms Land, Sea and Sky. The triadic cosmology observed by CRs. Ancient Celts swore their oaths by Land, Sea and Sky, and prayers that call upon the power of the three realms are found in the *Carmina Gadelica* and other collections of Gaelic prayer and poetry.

tine-éigean /tʹinʹə eːgʹən/ (I "Need-fire, fire of necessity")

Tír na nÓg /tʹiːr nə noːg/ (I "The Land of the Young") One of the most well-known Otherworld islands to the west, where the dead go and are believed to rest and grow young again.

toradh /torə/ (I "product"; SG *toradh* /torəɣ/ "consequence, effect") The "vital energy" in food, which is the portion consumed by the spirits when an offering is made, and which is said to drain out of food still on the vine by certain chronological points (usually *Oíche Shamhna*). Traditional lore states it is harmful, offensive, or at best non-nourishing to consume food once the *toradh* has gone out of it.

triads Verse/poetic form grouping three traditions, concepts, or precepts together. They have often been used as a mnemonic device in Celtic tradition and lore.

tríca cét /triːxə keːd/ (OI "thirty hundreds," pl. *tríca céta* /triːxə keːdə/) In ancient Irish terms, a household was reckoned at about thirty people per dwelling. A *tríca cét* was an area comprising one hundred households or, roughly, three thousand people.

túath /tuəθ/ (OI "tribe, people," pl. *túatha* /tuəθə/; I/SG *tuath* /tuə/ "country, territory" / "tenantry, country people") Historically, a *túath* consisted of a number of allied *tríca céta;* so a *túath* probably consisted of no less than 6,000 people. Probably a more accurate number for a *túath* would be no less than 9,000 people. There were said to be 250 *túatha* in ancient Ireland at the height of its prosperity.

Túatha Dé Danann /tuəθə dʹeː danəN/ (OI *túatha* "peoples, tribes, nations"; *Dé* gen. of *Dia*, "god"; *Danann* "of Dana/Danu [or

Ana/Anu]") The most well-known group of Irish divinities. They are said to be the penultimate inhabitants of the island of Ireland who, when defeated by the invading Milesians, retreated to the Otherworld (the Western Isles and the *síde* [fairy mounds]). In pseudohistorical sources they were said to be "world travelers," and later works of Christian theology treated them as supernatural beings who could be either "demonic" or "angelic." Well-known members of the Túatha Dé Danann include the three Goddesses of Ireland (Ériu, Fótla, and Banba), Brighid, the Dagda, Lugh and the Morrígan. The eponymous ancestress of this group is Danu or Anu.

Túatha Dé Domnann /tuəθə dʹeː dov(ə)nəN/ (OI *túatha* "peoples, tribes, nations"; *Dé* gen. of *Dia*, "god"; *Domnann* "of Domna/Domnu"?) See **Fomorian**.

Copyrights, Credits and Acknowledgements

The CR FAQ – An Introduction to Celtic Reconstructionist Paganism

Who created this document?

The CR FAQ was created collaboratively by regulars of the *Celtic Reconstructionist/Restorationist LiveJournal community (cr_r)*,[35] using a CeltiWiki database created for the project. The majority of the first-draft writing was done by Kathryn Price NicDhàna and Erynn Rowan Laurie.

Additional edits, refinements, and content were added by C. Lee Vermeers, Kym Lambert ní Dhoireann, Paul Pigman, Bob Daverin, Brenda Daverin, and Raven nic Rhóisín. The document was reviewed and commented on by the members of the cr_r community before publication, and their feedback was incorporated.

The authors would like to extend thanks to the cr_r community as a whole, and in particular to Dr. Phillip Bernhardt-House and Lisa Spangenberg for their academic corrections, Thomas Leigh for language assistance, Annelise Carson for additional book reviews, and Ogambear for his humor. Special thanks to Raven nic Rhóisín for hosting and managing the CeltiWiki.

---

[35] *http://community.livejournal.com/cr_r*

What is the purpose of this document?

The authors felt that a clear statement of many of the core beliefs of Celtic Reconstructionist Paganism would be useful to those seeking to understand or become more familiar with the religion.

Where will this document be archived?

The mother version is hosted at *http://www.paganachd.com/faq* and archived on the original CeltiWiki site.

For any errata and the most up-to-date version of the document, please visit *http://www.paganachd.com/faq*.

Copyright Notice

"The CR FAQ – An Introduction to Celtic Reconstructionist Paganism" – is Copyright ©2006 Kathryn Price NicDhàna, Erynn Rowan Laurie, C. Lee Vermeers and Kym Lambert ní Dhoireann. All copyrights are retained by the individual authors. Not to be reproduced without the express, written permission of the authors.

Information on the Print Edition

The hard copy/dead tree edition was prepared from the original CeltiWiki files between June, 2006 and July, 2007 by Paul Pigman for **River House Publishing**. Paul adapted the HTML, composing and indexing it for print using Microsoft® Word 2000 and Acrobat 6.0 Professional under Windows XP. The text was set in Gentium, a truly multilingual typeface pleasing to the eye and soothing to the Celtic soul.

The Pronunciation guide was written by Thomas Leigh, assisted by Kathryn Price NicDhàna. The Glossary was composed by Kathryn Price NicDhàna, Thomas Leigh, C. Lee Vermeers and Dr. Phillip Bernhardt-House, with additional content, feedback, coding and indexing by Paul Pigman; a couple of text additions were made by Kym Lambert ní Dhoireann and Erynn Rowan Laurie, and end-stage feedback was provided by Lierre Keith and Bob Daverin.

᪥ Copyrights, Credits and Acknowledgements ᪥

Paul Pigman would like to give special thanks to Kathryn Price NicDhàna and Thomas Leigh, without whom this book could not have happened. Kathryn organized the completion of the project, taking the lead on not only the writing and editing of the book itself, but also the herding-of-cats involved in organizing the contributors. In the course of the formatting and preparation of this book her contribution of sage advice, obsessive design pointers, perceptive criticism and terrifying insistence on working till she dropped was... *invaluable.* Our Gaelic Guru and Celtic Threat, Thomas Leigh, served as our esteemed and crucial language consultant. He repeatedly advised, clarified, fine-tuned, wrote, re-wrote, corrected our language mistakes with patience and good humour, and was available for panicked phone calls. If any language errors remain in the text, they are most certainly due to publisher's oversight or forgetting to ask for help.

On this note, Mr. Pigman assumes all responsibility for any mistakes or errors that may have been inadvertently introduced into the final result despite his feverish, assiduous and compulsive proofreading; it's an honor thing.

Index

www.ingramcontent.com/pod-product-compliance
Lightning Source LLC
Chambersburg PA
CBHW021228090426
42740CB00006B/436